AT THE TABLE OF THE KING

*" 'Man does not live on bread alone,
but on every word that comes from the mouth of God.' "
~ Matthew 4:4*

TRACI A. ALEXANDER

Revised edition, January 2012

Published by Trumpet and Torch Ministries, Inc.
Copyright © 2006, 2008, 2012 by Traci A. Alexander

All rights reserved. No portion of this book may be reproduced,
stored in a retrieval system, or transmitted in any form or by any means –
electronic, mechanical, photocopy, recording, scanning, or other –
except for brief quotations in critical reviews or articles,
without the prior written permission of the author.

ISBN: 978-1-938050-00-8

Unless otherwise indicated, Scripture quotations are from
the Holy Bible, New International Version,
copyright © 1973, 1978, 1984 by International Bible Society.

Scripture quotations identified KJV are from the King James Version.

To order additional copies of this resource write to:
Trumpet and Torch Ministries
P.O. Box 3327 Stafford, VA 22555
Order Online at www.trumpetandtorch.org
Email: info@trumpetandtorch.org

Printed in the United States of America

Dedication

To my Lord and Savior
Jesus Christ

*"When your words came,
I ate them;
they were my joy
and my heart's delight,
for I bear your name,
O LORD God Almighty."*
(Jeremiah 15:16)

You have taught me how to eat
and I have tasted and seen
how good the Lord is.

In You alone am I satisfied.

I have been emptied
and You have filled me up
with the only thing that matters –
more of You.

All I am is Yours.

You have given me everything
And I love You more than everything.

Thank You for inviting me
to feast from Your table.

Medical Disclaimer

The material contained in this book is written from a spiritual perspective. *Eat at the Table of the King* does not and is not meant to address the medical and physical aspects of fasting, instead it is intended to guide the reader into deeper dependence upon the Lord by developing the daily disciplines of "feasting" on the Word of God and prayer. This book is based, in part, upon the author's personal experiences and is provided for informational purposes only. The author is not a medical doctor and recommends that before beginning any type of fast, one should first consult a qualified health professional. For those with specific medical conditions, certain precautions and proper supervision by a physician may be needed before attempting a fast of any length.

Table of Contents

Preface..VII
Introduction..1
How to Use This Book..5
Fasting Commitment..8

Chapters

Week One
Hold Fast
11

Week Two
Stripping Leaves and Growing Roots
35

Week Three
Perseverance and Prayer
61

Week Four
Broken and Weak
85

Week Five
Finding Rest
111

Week Six
A Worthy Vessel
137

Conclusion..159

Appendices
A. Fasting Resolution..161
B. Fasting 101...162

C. Sources..167
D. Recommended Books on Fasting and Revival..168
E. Notes..169

Additional Blank Journal...170

⚜ Continue your Journey

Preface

"To the Church…, to those sanctified in Christ Jesus and called to be holy, together with all those everywhere who call on the name of our Lord Jesus Christ – their Lord and ours: Grace and peace to you from God our Father and the Lord Jesus Christ."
(1 Corinthians 1:2-3)

Dear Friend,

I write to you with praise and thanksgiving to God for showering us with His overwhelming love and constant care. As I pen these words, my mind is consumed with the numerous and daily ways the Lord reveals himself to us. He is forever pursuing us in order to lead us into a deeper and more intimate relationship with Him. His great mercy and grace have so shaped my life that I cannot help but be obedient to share with you the importance and urgency of spending time with our dear Father. The developing and maintaining of our personal relationship with Him must be our utmost priority.

I am encouraged by those of you who diligently seek to serve our Lord and desire to daily seek His face. Your faithfulness ensures that His name continues to be known throughout the world and that the fame of His renown continues throughout each generation. The testimony of so many of you, especially in the face of real and present evil, has encouraged and inspired my walk with the Lord.

At the same time, my heart breaks to hear of so many believers whose lives have taken an unfortunate, unnecessary, and undesirable turn. These believers have surrendered to the seduction of a fallen and temporal world instead of submitting to the power of the Holy Spirit who dwells inside them. Enticed by the world and its manipulative charms, the hearts and minds of many believers have been so captivated by the present rather than the eternal, they have let go of their first Love. Ensnared by the perceived need to achieve some worldly standard and held hostage by its weights and measures, some of God's servants have lost sight of their true home in Heaven. Others, beaten down by the difficulties and trials of this world, have wearily surrendered to the voices of destruction and disappointment. How discouraging that so many, saved by the Grace of our Lord Jesus Christ, do not even recognize the power instilled into their very beings by His Holy Spirit!

My heart aches over the way the enemy wins the daily battle in the lives of so many followers of Jesus Christ when, in fact, our Lord has come and already won the war! Remember that Jesus said, "I have told you these things, so that in Me you may have peace. In this world you will have trouble. But take heart! I have overcome the world." (John 16:33). He knew we would face obstacles and endure difficulties in this world, and He personally came to tell us not to be afraid, for He is with us now and is coming back for us soon. Today, as He prepares our glorious and eternal home, He is also preparing His servants here on earth for their final resting place with Him. In the meantime, our gracious Lord left His children an incomparable instruction Book to help us as well as His very Spirit to guide and comfort us.

Although we have this God-given empowerment, so many believers live in defeat instead of victory! The secular world is steadily gaining ground in the lives of believers, and it is stealing precious turf. Why is this happening? I believe this: we have become distracted by the busyness of life, and we have reduced the One who makes us His personal pursuit and priority to a box that we check (or not!) on our weekly to-do list. Instead of making the Lord our priority, we hurriedly run to Him at the end of a long and difficult week seeking a quick word of encouragement to sustain us through the next long and difficult week.

Unfortunately, just showing up on Sunday mornings does not convey to the Lord (or to anyone else!) that you love Him and that He is the utmost priority in your life; it merely says that He is a rote part of your weekly routine. Routines can become mundane, and we can quickly find ourselves checking out instead of checking in.

Our Heavenly Father desires – and deserves – so much more from us. He looks not for a list of our service projects, not for a roster of those whom we've helped, not for a tally of our church building fund contributions. Simply put, He looks for us. He wants time with us! So often, we cry out in the midst of our difficulty, "Where are You, God?" If we would just open our ears, we would hear Him reply, "I've been here all the time. Where have you been?" God listens when we cry out to Him, but, oh, how He desires us to spend time with Him! Even more, He wants us to want Him! He doesn't want our begrudged time; He wants our best time. We could avoid so much trouble – or we could walk peacefully through it – if we reconciled our time with the One who walks before us, behind us, and right beside us.

We live in very troubled times, and Jesus knew that we would. He desires that we be prepared for the everyday battles, not so we can fight them, but so we can face them, and, most importantly, so we can face them with the peace and assurance that He has gone before us, and He will guide us through. How can we walk with peace in this world if we live in anguish and fear? We can't. Peace comes only by putting our trust in the Lord Jesus and by being obedient to Him. We must weigh every decision on the scale of His Truth and view every moment from His eternal perspective.

The only way we can accomplish this is to daily read and study the Bible and to constantly pray and converse with our Heavenly Father. The greatest thing we can achieve in our lifetime is to grow more intimately and deeply in our relationship with the Lord. We will spend an eternity with Him, and it should be our heart's desire to know the One who loves us so much that He created us, and then came back and died for us so that we could live with Him forever.

Our time on this earth is short. We are not meant to grow roots here. Instead, we are to be grafted into the Vine of our Lord Jesus Christ in order to spread His love during our lifetime. My prayer for you, fellow believer, is that you set aside the pursuits of this world and, instead, pursue the Love of your life. *"But seek first His kingdom and His righteousness, and all these things will be given to you as well." (Matthew 6:33).*

Today is the day to start scheduling your life around your Lord instead of scheduling the Lord around your life. There are so many wonderful things to learn about your Savior as you read His Word, talk to Him, and spend time with Him. Your love for the Lord will grow exponentially as you begin to carve out precious time for Him throughout your day. He longs for fellowship with you; He is waiting for you! In the days and weeks ahead, I pray that you find your way back to your first Love, and, in turn, that you experience the love He has always desired you to know. You can find encouragement in the words of your Lord Jesus as He prayed for you in John 17.

Now, "To Him Who is able to keep you from falling and to present you before His glorious presence without fault and with great joy – to the only God our Savior be glory, majesty, power and authority, through Jesus Christ our Lord, before all ages, now and forevermore! Amen." (Jude 24-25).

Blessings for the journey,

Traci A. Alexander
Psalm 27

Introduction

*" 'Even now,' declares the LORD, 'return to Me with all your heart,
with fasting and weeping and mourning.' "*
(Joel 2:12)

We live in a fast-paced, self-service, convenience-oriented society. From sunrise to sunset, we are on the go and on the move. We want fast food, fast service, and fast answers. We spend our days e-mailing, text messaging, and downloading. We want what we want when we want it without expending much time, exerting much energy, or entailing much interaction. Our lives are a blur, and, if we pause for just a moment, if we stop for just an instant, if we reflect for even a second, we find ourselves completely overwhelmed and adrift in a sea of confusion and distraction.

Corrie ten Boom said it best when she articulated, "The devil finds great humor when we are up to our ears in work, but he trembles in fear when we pray." And he's laughing his head off. We are so distracted and busy with the act of living that we have lost all touch with our true priority. As believers, we have forgotten our First Love. Do you even remember what it was like? Can you recall the honeymoon stage when you first said "I do!" to your Savior and Lord? Can you recapture the light that shone in your eyes and the love that poured from your lips as you sang praises to Him for rescuing you from the muck and the mire, for setting you apart, and for giving you a divine purpose. How you rejoiced! You were the one laughing back then. The burden was lifted; the chains were loosened; the captive was freed. You wanted everyone to know that you were changed; you shared it with anyone who would listen!

How long did it last? Can you recollect what it felt like to be so in love – to yearn for every possible moment with Him, to sit at His feet, to commune and converse with Him. When did your light begin to fade? Is there not a weak flicker still keeping your faith alive? Do you desire to return to that place you once knew? Dare to remember that haven where you were safe, where burdens were light, and where worldly worries were irrelevant.

That place you long for is not far away. It's only the distance from your head to your heart. The price is your precious time, charged by every second, every minute, and every hour of your day. The path is composed of commitment and faith, but the world has set up roadblocks in an effort to keep you from reaching it.

In his book *Mere Christianity*, C.S. Lewis states "we are on enemy territory." Every morning when we get up and put our feet on the floor, we are walking in a mine field. Every step we take holds potential danger. Everywhere we turn, distraction looms. Every voice echoes potential discouragement. Flaming arrows fly from all sides; we just barely dodge them as we fly out of the door, speeding from one destination to another. If we've dared slip out of bed without putting on the proper armor, if we've breathed a single breath without consulting our Commander-in-Chief, we've laid ourselves bare and are ill-equipped to resist the strategic attacks aimed directly at us.

The enemy is gaining significant ground, not only in the lives of unbelieving followers, but also, and most distressingly, in the lives of believers for whom the victorious Christian life is but a faded memory. Having fallen prey to the deception of this world, we've become disoriented by living in a place that is not our home.

Set apart by our Father, we are here to do a job. He has given us a mission, but instead of waging the war, we've just pitched our tents. Our sights are not set on things above because we're so caught up in things below. We've adapted; we've accommodated; we've assimilated. We've done exactly what we've been warned not to do in Romans 12:2 – we've conformed to this world.

God is sending a warning to His children. He is urging us to awaken. He wants us to prepare for battle, to rise up out of our pit, to stand firm on His Word, and to trust Him for victory. He misses us; He loves us, and He's praying for us (John 17).

The enemy trembles most when we talk to God. When we humbly bow before our Lord, when we pray and seek His face (2 Chronicles 7:14), we employ our greatest tactical strategy. It's the greatest weapon we can wield to win the war in this enemy land. We need to attack the enemy where it hurts – on our knees! Running around indiscriminately, wearying ourselves with worry, and operating without His fuel will not win this war.

Today is the day to make a stand for what you believe! Today is the day to dirty your knees, to seek the Lord, to confess your sins, and to cry out for a land that is soon to see His judgment. Are there any faithful? Is there anyone to heed the call? I believe there are many, if not millions, whom God has sent a wake up call to. He woke me from my sleep, and I pray I never begin another day without hearing from Him and without seeking His face.

In *The Chronicles of Narnia*, Beaver said to Peter, "Aslan is on the move!" I believe that is true for this particular time in which we're living. God is on the move, and He is building His army, an army of faithful prayer warriors willing to fight His war moment by moment and battle by battle; His soldiers are in constant and fervent communion with their Father. Today, He is recruiting you. Take it one day at a time and one meal at a time. Begin by giving thanks to Him; progress by crying out to Him on behalf of all people and all nations "*in Jerusalem, and in all Judea and Samaria, and to the ends of the earth*" (Acts 1:8).

You've received a Divine invitation today to join God at His Holy table. Food is your most basic necessity. From the Garden of Eden, to manna from Heaven, to dining with sinners, to feeding the 5000, the Lord has always met this most basic need for His children. Throughout Scripture, food is used as an illustration to provide our essentials, to capture our attention, and to fuel our obedience. Think of the tree of the knowledge of good and evil where we first disobeyed Him; remember the shore of Galilee where He served breakfast and demonstrated His forgiveness. From the very beginning the Lord has desired that we seek Him for our source of food. If only we would trust Him, He would sustain us. Jesus admonished His followers in John 6:27 " '*Do not work for food that spoils, but for food that endures to eternal life, which the Son of Man will give you.*' " His desire is that we believe Him for the life He has planned for us.

There was a time in the Old Testament when food was sacrificed and given as an offering of repentance, honor, and praise. There are many instances throughout Scripture when food has been set aside completely for one day, three days, ten days, and forty days; those offerings supplemented humble prayer and petition to God for His help and mercy.

Today, we tend to set aside food only for the purpose of dropping a few pounds. We see food as a necessity for life, and yet, we've set aside the very One who gives us life. A wonderful opportunity exists for us to take God at His word and set aside our daily pursuit of filling our bellies and instead find nourishment for our hearts and our minds with the wholesome sustenance found only in His Word. " '*Therefore I tell you, do not worry about your life, what you will eat or drink; or about your body, what you will wear. Is not life more important than food, and the body more important than clothes?*' " (Matthew 6:25).

He holds your life in His hands – not just the life with which you're currently struggling but the life that He has planned and purposed for you – a life of victory and joy. To gain that life, however, requires sacrifice, time, belief, trust, obedience, and willingness.

We believe we are giving something up, when, in fact, a bountiful feast awaits us, and it offers more than we can ever imagine as well as a gracious abundance to share. You have the invitation, but you must choose to accept it. Won't you join Him at His banqueting table and receive a taste of what is to come? Choose one day at a time, one meal at a time, one tasty morsel at time, and one refreshing drink at a time.

But why fast? Is fasting some special key that unlocks the secrets of Heaven? Most of us are unfamiliar with fasting and have never been taught that it is an essential part of our Christian walk. It has, in fact, become a lost discipline in the past century. Yet, Jesus himself said, " *'When you fast . . .'* " (Matthew 6:16). Notice that he did not say, "if" you fast because He expected that we would fast. Scripture reveals that many of the greatest heroes acknowledged in the Bible were men and women who fasted and prayed. Moses, Elijah, Esther, Paul, and the Lord Jesus Himself fasted and prayed for a variety of reasons including, but not limited to, preparation for ministry and intercession for others. Some of the most significant movements in Christian history were led by people like Martin Luther and John Wesley who prayed and fasted. In most recent history, profoundly influential ministries led by Billy Graham, Bill Bright, and Charles Stanley all stemmed from men who faithfully sought the Lord's guidance through prayer and fasting.

The Lord desires to awaken us all to His plans and purposes, and fasting plays a major role in allowing us to hear the voice of God. Fasting teaches patience, humbleness, and reliance upon the Lord. It is in that quiet, restful, dependent place that we can hear from Him, and being in that place makes us willing to address the areas of our life that He reveals. God wants to use all of us, but He pursues those followers who are willing to submit and completely surrender to Him. In Psalms, He says, *"Be still, and know that I am God."* (Psalm 46:10a) Only in the place of quiet dependence on God will we recognize His true power and purpose; only there can we gain tremendous clarity for the work He is doing in this world.

Surrounded by so much disaster and destruction in this world, it is so easy to miss the fact that God is at work. He is sovereign, however, and He has already won the war. He wants to open our eyes and prepare our hearts to lead the next generation to faithfulness; He wants us to have the vision to see that He is preparing us for a much more wonderful place with Him.

If fasting clears our vision, tunes our hearing, stirs our passion, and fuels our hunger for more of God, if it makes us keen to accomplish His mission in this world, then we should be eager to accept His invitation to this most Holy dinner party. We have a Divine opportunity to sit at the table of Holy God and to dine with some of the greatest and most significant spiritual leaders in history. This invitation rivals any other, yet, instead of being moved and humbled by such an overture, we toss it aside as if to say, "Return to Sender, Address Unknown". We simply profess that such an invitation is not possible.

Apart from God, such an invitation is impossible, but, just like anything He summons us to do, if it is beyond our ability, then it must truly be from Him. The Lord does not assemble His invitation list with criteria such as outward appearance or ability. He sees your heart and engraves your name on His Holy invitation based simply upon your availability. If the Creator of the world says that you are worthy to dine at His table, then you should be nothing less than humbled and willing to accept His invitation.

The Lord extends His invitation to you just as you are – doubts, questions and all – and, once you're seated at His table, He will personally meet you there to share with you, to teach you, and to guide you. During your fast, you will find it amazing and enthralling to sit at His feet just as Mary did in the 10th chapter of Luke.

While you will not understand why He has called you, He will be faithful to lead you. During this time with the Lord, He will open your eyes to what He has planned, and you will become full – full of joy, full of hope, and full of expectancy. You will find yourself hungering for the next meal with Him. You will be satisfied yet starving for more. You will be yearning for more precious time with your Lord, and He will be pleased with you. He will take great delight in your desire to set aside everything else in order to spend time with Him.

We may not see the face of God while we live on this present earth, but we can certainly feel His favor when we please Him. He delights in our obedience and, at the end of this fast, the warmth of His light and the depth of His love will ignite your heart to serve Him – to go where He leads, to do what He asks, and to respond when He commands. If you are obedient, He will set you on a path to revive others, awakening them to what you yourself have been privileged to enjoy.

This is a Holy invitation, trimmed in His goodness and sealed with His love. You are the guest of honor at the table of the King of Kings! Anoint your head with oil, enter His courts with praise, and leave your shoes at the door for you are treading on Holy ground. Today, you will sit at the table of the Lord of Lords; you will sit face-to-face and talk intimately with Holy God, and you will gain access to a deeply personal and abiding relationship with your Heavenly Father.

If you are willing to accept Him at His Word, if you believe He keeps His promises, if you trust that He will lead you only to those paths of righteousness that will bring Him glory, then commit yourself right now to pray and to accept His invitation. Pull up your chair to His Holy table, and eat!

How to Use this Book

"Prayer and the Word are inseparably linked together.
Power of either depends on the presence of the other."
— Andrew Murray

When God called me to fast for 40 days in early 2006, I had no idea what I was doing or what I was getting myself into. I had never completed a 40-day fast, and I was not even aware that people did this kind of thing. I thought that something this radical was reserved only for the spiritual giants of the Bible, like Moses, Elijah, and Jesus. When I paused to truly consider that the Lord was calling me to do something that He Himself had done, I was completely humbled. Even still, I had many questions regarding how to begin, when to begin, what to do. I knew He had called me, but I had no other direction than "Go!"

I've walked with Jesus Christ as my Lord and Savior for over 28 years now, and I've found that God doesn't usually provide standard operating procedures for the tasks He assigns us. More often than not, we are given a command to go or to do, and we have nothing more than a deep longing to be obedient and an unsettled feeling that won't go away until we are. I knew what I was called to do, but all I had to guide me was faith to believe that what I heard from the Lord was true and trust to know that He would guide the way.

I believe that God gives us a task or a command to gauge our response. When His directive seems overwhelming or insurmountable (or both!), we must realize that the mission is not about us but about God revealing Himself to us. God loves to make Himself known in big and small ways. In the small things, we often miss Him completely. In the big things, we are often too afraid to even risk seeing Him at work. God is all around us desiring to show Himself to us, and we are either too busy to notice or too afraid to see.

I knew this journey would require complete trust in the Lord. I had seen Him work so many times before in my life. Why should this time be any different? Still, the unknown is always a little frightening. In Joshua 1:9, God reassures us to be strong and courageous for He is with us everywhere we go. So, I took His promise to heart and mustered up enough courage to believe Him for one day, and guess what? He did not leave me hanging! He met me right where I was. In His word, He showed Himself; when I was on my knees, He listened; during my daily walk, He was with me; when I was weak, He picked me up and encouraged me. I made the choice to get up every morning and read His word, and, in the afternoon, I realized that I needed a Holy time-out with Him. In the evenings, when I was tired and weak, I held on tighter and cried out to Him all the more.

There were many times that I felt alone on this journey. I started researching books on fasting, trying to understand what others experienced. What I found was a lot of information on fasting and some great stories about fasting, but I didn't find much instruction or guidance. God led me to some books and devotionals that helped me along the way, but, as I neared the end of my fast, God laid something else on my heart: the need to encourage others who would answer the call to sit at His table and eat with Him.

This book is just that: a daily meal plan, a daily devotional, a simple guide book to help you as you begin your journey into the discipline of fasting. It is designed for both praying and for reading God's Word – they work together. Each day is organized with a devotional for every meal. There are Scriptures to read, words to encourage you, excerpts from my own fasting journal, and space to record your own prayers and to journal your own thoughts as God leads you through each day from meal to meal. I encourage you to journal, to record the challenges and triumphs of each day, to write the names of the people whom God lays on your heart so that you can pray for them, and to pour out your own prayers in written form to your Father. The journals that I have kept over the years encourage me and constantly remind me of God's faithfulness and guidance over the years. Your journaling in this book will serve as your own record of God's revelations to you during this time. He wants to work in you and through you in the coming days, weeks, and months, and He will use this preparation time to begin revealing His plans and purposes for your life.

Fasting is completely voluntary, and your decision to fast and to believe God for it is entirely between you and Him. At the beginning of the first chapter, you will find a Fasting Commitment to complete and sign. It is a personal commitment between you and God regarding the length and the details of your personal fast. I felt a strong call to go the entire 40 days with the Lord on liquids only. He may call you to do otherwise. You should pray and seek the Lord's direction for this journey. As well, you should consider any physical or medical conditions that may need to be addressed. (Please see the Fasting 101 section located in the appendix of this book for further information about the types of fasts and how to begin your fast). When you finish *Eat*(ing), you will find a Fasting Resolution at the end of the last chapter. In retrospect, my agreement at the beginning of the fast was based on my own desires, fears, and lack of understanding. By the end of my fast with the Lord, however, my resolution looked totally different than my original commitment! I marvel now at the record of my thoughts in the beginning; how amazing to see, in writing, my first baby steps of believing God for His call to fast and then to see the way He transformed me, revealed Himself to me and accomplished His intentions within me. Had I any idea at all what God wanted to show me or what He was capable of, I would have written something totally different at the beginning of my fast. Now, though, I have an amazing and personal example to encourage me for every future step of obedience that the Lord requires.

Eat includes 40 days of devotionals, but not everyone is called to such a radical fast. It is an amazing step of faith to believe God for even one day or one meal. With every step of the fast, however, just as in your overall life's journey, God will show Himself more faithfully and reveal Himself more clearly as you draw nearer to Him and walk in closer cadence with Him. The greatest thing you can do is just be willing to believe Him; surrender, and let Him guide you where He wants to take you. You may decide to take one day with Him while He may guide you to go three. You may decide to fast for seven straight days; He may guide you instead to fast one day each week. Whatever your commitment, it is between you and God. Whatever your journey, I pray that this book will be a source of encouragement. Even if you don't fast for the full 40 days, plan to use the daily devotionals and the journal space each day. The main purpose is to draw you into a deeper, more abiding relationship with Jesus Christ as you grow in the knowledge of Him.

If you do fast the full 40 days, you will find it challenging. It will not be easy – it is not meant to be. God can reveal in a 40-day fast what it often takes a lifetime for us to see. As you proceed through the six weeks, you will find that each of the six chapters follows a specific process through which the Lord will take you from the beginning to the end of the fast. The Lord will use this discipline of spending time with Him three times a day to develop in you a greater dependence upon Him. To accomplish this, He will gently peel back your layers and break apart those things that have become a wall around your heart. He will then rebuild you into His treasured masterpiece, and you will experience a time of quiet rest sweetened with indescribable joy, and, in the end, you will have a renewed vision to accomplish His great purposes in your life.

The days and weeks ahead will not be without battles and temptations. It will be an intensely personal journey. But, it will be more than you can imagine and beyond anything you can fathom. I've learned that if you're willing, if you make yourself available, God will meet you right where you are, and He has Divine plans to do great things in you and through you. It is for His glory that you be made fully His. In this journey, you will be weakened, you will be emptied, you will be vulnerable, and you will be broken. But, you will also be filled and given strength. God will recreate you piece by piece into a purified and more useful vessel. A new passion for serving Him and for seeking Him will become the sustenance that satisfies you.

Your commitment to fast doesn't have to end with the 40 days. I have remained committed to fasting at least one day each week, and I continue to use this journal for my own daily devotionals. My heart is committed to living the fasted lifestyle – a life of full devotion to the Lord. He has become my utmost priority and my great desire is to live in obedience to Him every day of my life. We are each responsible for listening to our Master's voice. I pray you have found peace in the quiet times with Him and have learned to discern that still small whisper He is speaking to your heart. If you have found this journey has blessed your life, I pray you will share it will others. If you would feel led to live the fasted lifestyle, pray about continuing your journey online at www.trumpetandtorch.org where you will find this journey, as well as, additional 40-day journeys and other prayer and fasting devotionals. In the next 40-day journey, *WELLSPRING: Unleash Your Passion for God*, you take your new found intimacy in Christ and unleash it into a life of obedience to the Lord (a list of additional prayer and fasting devotionals are listed under the "Continue Your Journey" section of this book). I would love to hear about your experience, and I will be praying for you as you join countless others before you by stepping out in faith to experience the power and discipline of fasting with the Lord.

God bless you!

My Personal Commitment to Fast & Pray

" 'I am the Living Bread that came down from heaven. If anyone eats of this bread, he will live forever. This bread is My flesh, which I will give for the life of the world.' "
(John 6:51)

Today, I, _____, am learning to eat, spiritually. When I was a baby, drinking milk seemed like the most natural thing to do, but, as I grew up, I fought hard against the choices put in front of me. I turned up my nose at things on my plate that I had never seen before. I spit out those things that didn't taste good to me, and I refused to eat what I didn't like. In those things I did enjoy – I overindulged. Sometimes, I just couldn't resist; I consumed more than I needed and found myself painfully uncomfortable. Over time I became burdened and weighed down by the concerns of this world. I grew complacent with little desire or energy to change. I was aware that my spiritual health was at risk and that I was contributing little of eternal significance. I realize I have been too self-focused and am not making the impact for God's Kingdom that I desire. I have the Holy Spirit living inside me, yet I am not living the victorious and abundant Christian life that God has purposed for me.

Today, however, I am willing to take a few baby steps towards, and at, the direction of my Heavenly Father. For today, I will pursue the life that He intends for me to live – a life full of devotion to Him. I realize that this declaration is just the beginning of a very long journey. I know that I do not have control over some of the circumstances that will surround me, but I understand that I do have control of my responses to them. Today, I am responding to the Lord's call to sit at His table; I am accepting His invitation to dine with Him. I will not fear those things that I do not recognize or understand. I am willing to accept whatever my Father serves; I will eat whatever He puts on my plate, because He is God. He knows exactly what I need. He has made all things, including me, and **"in all things God works for the good of those who love Him, who have been called according to His purpose" (Romans 8:28)**. I desire to savor every morsel that He feeds me, and I will accept His nourishment for the good of my spiritual health. I wish to sit at His table and talk with Him, to share my struggles and ask Him for help, to gain His wisdom and guidance, to offer my gratitude and give Him thanks, to get to know Him better and draw closer to His presence, to be wrapped in His love and to accept Him at His Word. I yearn to be called His friend, and I long to make the most of every opportunity to eat with Him.

Teach me, dear Lord, one day at a time, and one meal at a time. I long to talk with You each day. Moment by moment, help me remember to call on You – not only in times of trouble but also in opportunities of praise, worship, and gratitude. I am willing, Lord, to seek You and to spend time with You.

My personal agreement to dine with the Lord is as follows: (Record your current standing in your walk with the Lord. Address your concerns about this fast. Communicate what you believe the Lord is calling you to do (i.e. length of this fast, the type of fast). Write your own prayer to the Lord as you begin your journey.

_____
_____
_____
_____
_____
_____
_____
_____
_____
_____
_____
_____
_____
_____
_____
_____
_____
_____
_____
_____
_____
_____
_____
_____

Heavenly Father, I long to see where You will take me these next 40 days. I will not listen to the voices of discouragement when I fail. I will clean my plate, wipe the crumbs off of my face, and try again at my next meal. This is a journey – a moment-by-moment process. I am willing to learn and wanting to grow. My desire is for more of You and for less of me. I have already made a commitment to you as my Savior; today, I commit to you as my Sustainer.

Signature: _____

Date: _____

*"Now choose life, so that you and your children may live and that you may
love the LORD your God, listen to His voice and hold fast to Him.
For the LORD is your life, and He will give you many years . . ."*
(Deuteronomy 30:19b-20)

I am an avid reader, and a common thread seems to run through many of the authors whose works I enjoy. They all write that today's Christians are not living the fully surrendered, committed, and victorious Christian life. The world today, I believe, offers so many distractions. In the midst of them, our attention is easily divided; we quickly become busy and overwhelmed, and we have little or no margin in our lives. The essence of our Christian walk – an unwavering and nurturing relationship with the Lord – is relegated to a forgotten corner and shelved for our future convenience.

Oh, we've accepted the Lord as our Savior; we have sealed our eternal destination. But, then, we've just impassively moved on with the matter of living. The problem is, as the previous verse states, when we choose God, we choose life. He is our life; He holds our very being in His hands. But, onto what are we holding? Are we holding on to the hope of the next job promotion or the next bigger, newer, more expensive house? Are we hanging on to destructive relationships or to disappointing and unfulfilling habits? Are we clawing for dreams that continually slip through our fingers and for wishes that just seen to fade away? We cling desperately to the things of this world; in our limited and distorted vision, they're the only things that seem available and attainable. Yet, when we open our hands, we find nothing for which we've labored and toiled. Here's the truth we're missing: God has called us to "hold fast" to Him…only to Him.

Your hands are meant to toil the earth, but your heart is meant to wrap around Him! Your life is meant to be lived by daily seeking Him, by enjoying His gifts, and by desiring to spend time with Him as much as He desires to spend time with you.

As in our eating habits, though, we've made some unhealthy decisions about life in general, and we've established some dreadfully unsound routines. Our choices provide us with way too many empty calories; we fill ourselves, but we receive little or no nourishment.

This week, as you go about your daily routine, your stomach, at some point, will begin to growl in protest that it's time to stop and refuel. Instead of lining up in the drive-thru while you're on your cell phone, multi-tasking so as not to waste a single moment of "your" time, just stop. Pull off of the road, and park yourself. Find a quiet place alone. Go to the One who holds the clock of eternity in His hands; go to the Author and Creator of time, and ask Him to extend the minutes of your day as your offer and surrender them to your Lord. What you put in your belly will never sustain you like what you store in your heart. Let this devotional guide you to His Word. Take a bite of His daily bread. Savor every morsel that the Lord gives you. Remember, *"They are not just idle words for you – they are your life."* (Deuteronomy 32:47a).

Talk to the Lord, and tell Him about your next appointment. Commit to Him your concerns for the day. Share with Him your burdens. Offer Him gratitude for this precious moment alone with Him. Feel your stomach become full as He lifts the weight from your shoulders and clears the confusion from your mind. You will face the next few hours much stronger, more focused, more relaxed and better equipped. How much longer until your next meal with Him? Let go of the day's toil, and hold fast to the Lord.

"But be very careful to keep the commandment and the law that Moses the servant of the LORD gave you: to love the LORD your God, to walk in all His ways, to obey His commands, to hold fast to Him and to serve Him with all your heart and all your soul."
(Joshua 22:5)

DAY 1
Learning to Eat

Breakfast

"I need Thee, O I need Thee, every hour I need Thee!
O bless me now, my Savior—I come to Thee!"
— Hawks

⚜ **Daily Bread** – Read: Romans 12:1-2

"Today is the first day of my fast. The Lord has been impressing upon my heart to take this journey with Him, but I haven't been able to figure out how to do a complete 40-day fast while still taking care of my husband, my three children, and all the activities that we are involved in that require social eating. I don't want to appear rude, and I don't want anyone to be asking a lot of questions. I want this to be a deeply personal and spiritual journey because I know that God has so much to reveal to me about the current path He has me on. Is it possible, Lord, to accomplish this in the midst of living everyday life? I have so many questions. I've never done this before. Can it be done? I believe you are the God of the impossible. I know 'I can do all things through Christ who gives me strength.' (Philippians 4:13). But this? This is just so far out of my understanding. I guess that gives me all the more reason to trust You. You've taken me through so much. I've believed You in so many other unknown places. So, today is the day I choose to believe You for this. I'll go where you lead, but I'm only agreeing to one meal at a time for now…"(My Fasting Journal, Day 1).

It's been said that breakfast is the most important meal of the day. Yet, many of us are in such a hurry to get out of the door and on with the day's events that we just skip right over it. Even with children in the home, very few families take the opportunity to sit and pray together around the breakfast table to prepare for the day ahead. Our family is no different. We are off and running from the moment the alarm sounds. We quickly jump headstrong into the day's battles without pausing to realize that we are inadequately dressed for them, and we find ourselves ill-prepared to stand against impending danger.

We spend so much time thinking about our physical attire, making sure that our outer appearance is perfect, but we fail to adequately prepare our hearts and minds for the day. We don't need a masterful plan; we don't even need to have it all figured out. But, we must submit to the Master Himself who already knows the plans He has for us.

This may be called a fast, but take it slowly as you advance one moment, one meal, one verse, and one prayer at a time. Let God do the work that food can not do, and savor every morsel that He gives you.

What consumes your mind today? For whom can you pray? Take time to journal your thoughts and prayers now and each day at each meal.

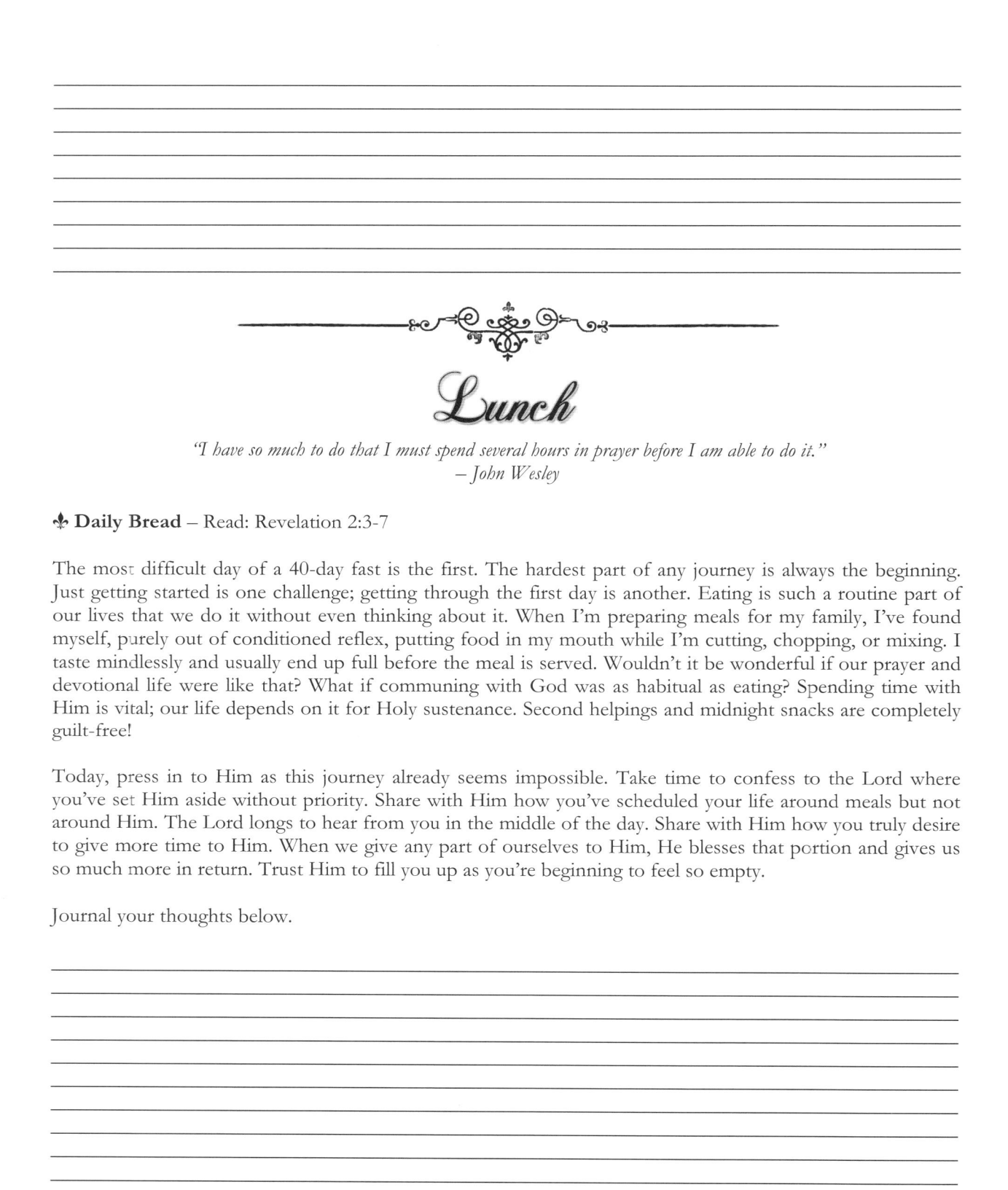

Lunch

"I have so much to do that I must spend several hours in prayer before I am able to do it."
— *John Wesley*

⚜ **Daily Bread** – Read: Revelation 2:3-7

The most difficult day of a 40-day fast is the first. The hardest part of any journey is always the beginning. Just getting started is one challenge; getting through the first day is another. Eating is such a routine part of our lives that we do it without even thinking about it. When I'm preparing meals for my family, I've found myself, purely out of conditioned reflex, putting food in my mouth while I'm cutting, chopping, or mixing. I taste mindlessly and usually end up full before the meal is served. Wouldn't it be wonderful if our prayer and devotional life were like that? What if communing with God was as habitual as eating? Spending time with Him is vital; our life depends on it for Holy sustenance. Second helpings and midnight snacks are completely guilt-free!

Today, press in to Him as this journey already seems impossible. Take time to confess to the Lord where you've set Him aside without priority. Share with Him how you've scheduled your life around meals but not around Him. The Lord longs to hear from you in the middle of the day. Share with Him how you truly desire to give more time to Him. When we give any part of ourselves to Him, He blesses that portion and gives us so much more in return. Trust Him to fill you up as you're beginning to feel so empty.

Journal your thoughts below.

"God does not hold me responsible for success, but for faithfulness."
– A missionary speaking to Corrie ten Boom

⚜ **Daily Bread** – Read: Isaiah 55

As the end of the day approaches, you realize that you haven't eaten, and the enemy begins his full-force attack. Your head hurts, and your temper is short. Cling to the verses you've read today. Think about how much better you were prepared for the day's pressures because you intentionally paused to read God's word and talk with Him this morning and throughout the day. Have you already had some victories? Have you seen His hand in your day? Did you find that you had more opportunity to accomplish your tasks because you surrendered your time to Him?

Before each day has ended, I often find occasion to use the verse of Scripture that was given to me that very morning. Perhaps I offer it as a word of encouragement to a friend, or, it may be a helpful reminder to guard my own thoughts and actions.

Congratulations! You've made it through the toughest part of the journey: Day One. Take time to journal your thoughts as you complete your first day of fasting. Thank God for what He has already shown you, and record what you are anticipating in the days to come.

_____
_____
_____
_____
_____
_____
_____
_____
_____
_____
_____
_____
_____
_____
_____
_____
_____
_____
_____
_____
_____
_____
_____
_____
_____

Day 2: Fuel for the Fast

Breakfast

"You will seek Me and find Me when you seek Me with all your heart."
(Jeremiah 29:13)

⚜ **Daily Bread** – Read: Jeremiah 29:11-14

I started my fast not really knowing what it was all about. Today is a good day to see what the Scriptures say about the subject, and a good place to start is the 58th chapter of Isaiah which details the kind of fasting God does – and does not – desire. Take a few moments to familiarize yourself with that chapter.

Fasting was an important discipline in the Old Testament and was often used by God's people to cry out to Him for His mercy and protection. Fasting was also observed by those praying to discern God's will and to prepare for His service. Our Lord Jesus set the example for us when He, Himself, fasted at the onset of His earthly ministry "to demonstrate His absolute dependence upon the Father." Following are some fasts (a few of many!) recorded throughout the Scriptures:

1 Samuel 7:6 – for the Israelites to be delivered.

Ezra 8:21-23 – for protection while carrying the temple items.

Esther 4:16 – to save her people from destruction.

Acts 9:9 – when God gave Saul new eyes to see and a new vision for his life's mission.

Acts 13:2-3 – at the beginning of Paul and Barnabas' ministry to the Gentiles.

Acts 14:23 – for the selection of the Elders appointed by Paul and Barnabas.

The Scriptures tell us the reason the Lord honors our fasting: *"If My people, who are called by My name, will humble themselves and pray and seek My face and turn from their wicked ways, then I will hear from heaven and will forgive their sin and will heal their land." (2 Chronicles 7:14).*

As you fast, you are joining hundreds of faithful followers and saints of the Bible who stood up for their nation and their people and who cried out for God's help when no one else was willing. Because of their faithfulness and willingness to humble themselves by fasting and praying, the Lord showed His mercy, healed their sickness, and delivered their people from His judgment.

Our nation is in crisis; our world is sick, starving for God's mercy, and, we, His children, have lost our first Love. Fasting is the pathway to deeper intimacy with God; it is an awakening of our hearts to the hungry and helpless in the world, and it's an opportunity for the Lord to bless us like we've never known. It is a Holy privilege to answer the call to fast! Take advantage of your dining time with the Lord. You're not skipping meals for the purpose of creating time to accomplish your many tasks. The purpose of these precious moments is to help you focus on Whom and what is truly important. Reading God's word, communing, and communicating with Him are your highest priorities.

I pray that this breakfast was both filling and fulfilling and that you feel more committed to this banquet in which the Lord has invited you to partake. Humble yourself, pray, and seek His face each day.

___

Lunch

"Feed your faith – that starves your doubt to death."

⚜ **Daily Bread** – Read: John 6:51-58

The Lord is so good when we seek Him! He will never fail us and will always give us just what we need just when we need it. As I prayed to Him and asked for more insight about the discipline of fasting, the Lord led me to a friend who had fasted years before and who had collection of books on the subject. God always wants to supply our needs, and, on this day, He supplied not only my need of knowledge but also a friend with whom to share my journey.

The Scriptures tell us, in Matthew 6:16, not to fast as the hypocrites did. They wanted everyone know to about their fasting and about the great sacrifice that they were making. Everything for which God calls us is purposed to build up His body in Christ and is not meant to show off our individual participation. There is a huge divide, however, between pretension and apprehension, and God calls us to stand in that gap between self-importance and self-consciousness. Simply put, we must be humble but not hidden. Humility is the root of all fasting, but the enemy would like us to believe that humility means privacy. Although this fast is deeply personal, and the Lord has things He specifically wants to show you, His desire is that you ultimately share the great work He is doing in your life in order to build others up and encourage them in their faith.

Pray that the Lord will help you discern those with whom you can share your fasting journey. Ask for others to join you or to pray for you. The Lord Jesus Himself shares in your pilgrimage; He spent 40 days in the desert fasting and praying before beginning His public ministry. Reading about His tests and trials in the 4th chapter of Matthew will embolden you to persevere. He will surround you with love, hope, and reassurance as you diligently seek Him, and, as confirmation that you are walking in His will, He will also surround you with people who will pray for you and encourage you in your obedience.

Has the Lord given you a gift today – a book, a phone call from a friend, an answer to a prayer? Praise Him for all the ways He daily reveals Himself to you! If you have not received the kind of encouragement for which you've hoped, look outward, and pray for others who also need uplifting or others who are also fasting.

Dinner

"I can't store up good feelings and behaviors – but only draw them fresh from God each day."
– Corrie ten Boom

⚜ **Daily Bread** – Read: Hebrews 12:1-3

The first few days of fasting will prove to be very challenging. You are learning to change old habits and to develop new ones. You are recognizing the busy routine of your life and discovering the importance of making the Lord your first priority. Eating is the simplest human function; it's often taken for granted and abused with unhealthy habits. When you choose to dine with the Lord, you are learning to eat in a new way. After a meal with Him, you will feel satisfied yet hungry for more. You will learn that you can never get enough of Jesus, and you'll never walk away from Him empty.

As today winds down, remember how God has shown Himself in big and small ways. Consider how He's comforted you and filled you as you've pressed through the hunger pains and the headaches. It's just as important to fix your eyes on Jesus late in the day as it is early in the morning. The enemy is still on the prowl, and the darkness is his hiding place.

Praise God for the way He provides for you and protects you; thank Him for the example both He and His Word have given you.

Day 3
Losing Control

Breakfast

" 'The Spirit is willing, but the body is weak.' "
(Matthew 26:41b)

⚜ **Daily Bread** – Read: Matthew 26:36-46

"I woke up this morning with a headache, and I was lightheaded. I recognized immediately that I was consumed with myself and my pains, and I was already beginning to lose focus. This fast is about redirecting my focus to the Lord. It's about making Him my priority regardless of how I feel or the circumstances I'm in. Lord, help me to fill my mind with your words and only with thoughts of You. Let the pain and the ache become the result of so diligently seeking You that I become dizzy with the awesome wonder of how great You truly are. Amen." (My Fasting Journal, Day 3).

It's the third day of your fast, and your body is realizing that this not the way you usually do things. It will begin to protest, and you will feel it. The enemy will invade your mind and tell you that this is not wise, not healthy, not natural. But this is not a natural journey; it is a supernatural one.

As your body grows weak, as you receive fleshly signals of pain and difficulty, as you begin to hear voices of discouragement, stop and pray. Pray against the temptation to quit, the temptation to lose control, and the temptation to stay in bed. Follow Jesus' example when He fasted in the desert.

Try to focus beyond the distraction of your body's rebellion, and realize that this is new to your body as well as to your mind and to your spirit. Give your body time to accept the changes that will occur; this time will pass. Remember that in and through all circumstances, God calls us to believe Him and to have faith that He is in command even when everything else seems out of control.

As you read His Word, pray and release to the Lord those areas of your life that are unruly and unmanageable. Ask Him to reveal any areas in your life which you have not yet submitted to Him. Pray that He will help you release control but not lose control.

_____
_____
_____
_____
_____
_____
_____

"To escape temptation, flee to God."

⚜ **Daily Bread** – Read: 1 Peter 4:7-8

When we are in pain, we often lash out in anger at the people around us. Very few of us are properly geared to be proactive when it comes to suffering. We wait until the grief is upon us, and then we react. This afternoon, as you are confronted with problems and issues with your family, friends, co-workers and committee members, remain clear-minded and self-controlled even if your head pounds.

Be aware of those around you who tend to exhibit a lot of anger and who tend to push people away with cruel words, negative attitudes and constant criticism. Rather than taking their outbursts personally, try to see them from a different perspective. Consider the pain that surely shrouds them; they must be hurting if they are lashing out indiscriminately, slinging their misery on everyone around them. See their anger as a plea. "Feel my pain!" is what they are really saying. Recognize that the Lord may have specifically chosen you to accept them and stand by them when everyone else has seemingly rejected and discarded them.

People deal with pain in many different ways, but it is important to stand firm and face it head-on whether you're persevering through your own or standing by someone else's. During your lunch break today, pray through your own pain, and ask for an extra dose of self-control. Pray, too, for those whose pain is so vocalized and so toxic that you just don't want any part of it; ask God for an abundance of compassion as well as for the energy, wisdom, and courage to care for His hurting children.

Dinner

"For out of the overflow of the heart the mouth speaks."
(Matthew 12:34b)

⚜ **Daily Bread** – Read: Proverbs 15:1-8

Dinner time provides a great opportunity to share with your spouse, your children, and your friends. It's a chance to reflect on the day and to celebrate one another's victories. Within that safe arena, we learn respect for one another, we delight in one another's accomplishments, and we encourage one another in the midst of difficulties.

Our words, kind or otherwise, are very powerful. I personally have spent years chewing and choking on the words of rotten fruit meant to discourage me, but God desires that we diligently and consistently study His Word which is a feast of life and hope! His Word does not maim, kill, or destroy like the destructive words of the enemy. The enemy represents death and destruction while the Lord radiates life.

Jesus is called the Word. He came to bring life to all who would hear, listen, and believe. The Holy Bible overflows with His life-giving words, and no physical food can feed or nourish us as His words can. Words first form in our thoughts before later spilling out of our mouths. We are all guilty of thinking and speaking unkind words, and we must be more conscious and deliberate about what we allow to enter our minds. We must filter our thoughts before they land on our tongues.

Tonight, as you close the door on another day, reflect on the words you uttered today. Did you offer a word of encouragement to someone? Did you speak in anger to anyone? Did you cut someone down or lift someone up? Pray about the areas in which you need to improve, and ask the Lord to show you how to better communicate with those who prove difficult to love.

_____
_____
_____
_____
_____
_____
_____
_____
_____
_____
_____
_____
_____
_____
_____
_____
_____
_____
_____
_____

Look up your favorite scripture and meditate on each word. Let the beauty and truth of that passage roll around on your tongue, and taste its sweetness. Take time to thank God for the way His Word gives you exactly what you need exactly when you need it.

My favorite Scripture is:
_____
_____
_____

It has helped me in the following way(s):

Setting the Pace

Breakfast

"Whatever is your best time in the day, give that to communion with God."
— Hudson Taylor

⚜ **Daily Bread** – Read: 2 Timothy 4:1-8

"God has allowed us a set amount of time to bring light into this lost and dying world. How can we be a brilliant light of hope when we sit in darkness and struggle over the depths of our own sinfulness and despair? There is so much available to us and so much God has planned and purposed for us; if we could just hold on to hope, and take a leap of faith, and trust Him for tomorrow – or even just for the next step or the next moment. We don't have to figure it all out. He has already worked it all out. We just need to walk it out. We should do a little faith walk every now and then, and see how much stronger our spiritual legs will become. We know that we get stronger when we exercise. We know we gain energy when we eat right. Our fuel for living is the Word of God." (My Fasting Journal, Day 4).

It's been said that a journey of a thousand miles begins with just a single step. To get anywhere, we need to put one foot in front of the other, and keep on moving. The journey of life is a long and difficult one. It is challenging and tiring, but we must persevere. There is a finish line; there is a reward, but we must press on to the cross and face our Holy Lord to receive it.

Are you questioning the length of this race? Submit all of your doubts to the Lord whether they pertain to life in general or just to this particular fast. Four days out of forty seems like a drop in the proverbial bucket, but, just as there is a reward waiting for you at the end of this life, there is also a reward waiting for you at the end of this fast. Jesus is holding your prize; He's rooting you on, and He's your biggest supporter.

Don't think of taking one step without the Lord today; consider Him your personal trainer. Cast your cares upon Him; He's waiting to lighten your load so that you are free to run the race that He's set before you.

_____
_____
_____
_____
_____
_____

Lunch

"Blessed is the man who perseveres under trial, because when he has stood the test, he will receive the crown of life that God has promised to those who love Him."
(James 1:12)

⚜ **Daily Bread** – Read: James 1:2-4

Have you ever trained for a marathon? Do you know anyone who has? My brother loves that type of cruel bodily punishment. I am amazed at the training and discipline required to prepare for this type of long-distance race. Practice is constant for days and weeks; a very specific regimen of food and drink keeps the body fueled and hydrated. The training is exact, and the pressure is enormous.

It's interesting that no matter how hard one trains for these races, the outcome can never be predicted. At the very least, a runner can count on, at some point, actually crossing the finish line. My oldest brother recently competed in a marathon and hurt his leg early in the race. He continued to struggle through the pain, and he did finish the race. His time may not have exceeded his expectations, but he did accomplish his goal of completing the race.

In life, we can also exercise faithfully, train diligently, eat healthy, and, generally, take good care of ourselves, but we can never predict when we will stumble, fall, get hurt, or get sick. We can be sure, however, that at some point, we will endure hardship and pain. Knowing that difficulty is inevitable should not slacken or hinder our efforts; it should make us all the more concerned about being properly prepared when calamity strikes. We should be persistent in our efforts to gain strength and to remain healthy, but no amount of physical training can give us what spiritual training can. We must be alert to our areas of weakness; they are open targets for the enemy, and we must be willing to address any areas where we lack self-control.

To set the pace, we must have a game plan supported by a diligent training program. Ask God to reveal the weaknesses that warrant your special attention. Be willing to follow His strategy, and trust Him as your Coach. He'll guide you into shape, so you'll have endurance for the race He has placed before you. Hebrews 12:1 encourages *"…let us run with perseverance the race marked out for us."* It's not enough just to start well; you must also finish well.

Dinner

"My Bible to me is a guidebook true that points for my feet the way. That gives me courage and hope and cheer and guidance for every day."
— Anonymous

⚜ **Daily Bread** – Read: Isaiah 30:21

Have you ever left on a trip without a map or a clear set of directions? I like to know exactly where I'm going, and, the more detailed the instructions, the better! The Bible is a great map for life. Extremely detailed, it paints a beautiful picture of our final destination, Heaven. The only way to get there, as the Bible tells us, is through believing Jesus. The Bible exceeds the simple directions that you find in a typical road map. Instead, this lavishly illustrated Guide fleshes out its instruction with words of encouragement, stories of others who have traveled the same route before us, and explanations for handling any obstacles or roadblocks that threaten to hinder the progress of our journey. Throughout the Bible, graciously planted landmarks let us know that we're traveling in the right direction and reassure us that, if we just keep our eyes set on Jesus, we will make it to our eternal destination.

Many Christians claim that they don't know God's will for their life, that they can't discern God's direction for their path. The more time you spend reading and studying the Scriptures, the more He will reveal, confirm, and direct your steps. This fast is an opportunity to gain clearer direction from Him. If you honestly and diligently seek Him daily, if you take Him at His word for every meal, and if you are willing to accept the work He is doing in you, as well as the work that He's preparing for you to do, then you will get the answers you are seeking.

What questions do you have for the Lord tonight?

Day 5
More than Bread

Breakfast

" '...Is not life more important than food...?' "
(Matthew 6:25)

⚜ **Daily Bread** – Read: Deuteronomy 8:3

By now, your body should be used to your new routine of not fueling it with food, and, hopefully, you've established a habit of substituting God's Word as your sustenance.

I keep a small Bible in my purse, and I am amazed at the many opportunities throughout the day that I have to read it. Just five-minute nibbles here and there, throughout the day, can fill me up! When I'm stalled in traffic, sitting in the doctor's office, waiting for a friend, or biding time while my children are at dance lessons and sporting events, I tear into His word for a morsel or two.

It doesn't take much time, and every page offers words of hope, guidance, and encouragement. Jesus called us to live, and He came to us so that we would live more abundantly (John 10:10). Living the abundant life, though, doesn't mean eating well, exercising more, and trying to extend your life with artificial preservatives. It's about living your life more fully in Him. It's about seeking opportunities to indulge in His word and to feast upon His truth. It's about emptying yourself, pouring out your concerns and troubles to your Father, offering Him your praise and worship, so that you will be refilled and refueled with nothing but His power, mercy, and grace.

Ask God to give you plenty of moments today to snack on His Word. Carry your Bible with you wherever you go, and don't be afraid to use it.

___
___
___
___
___

Lunch

" 'Therefore, I tell you, do not worry about…what you will eat or drink…' "
(Matthew 6:25)

⚜ **Daily Bread** – Read: 1 Corinthians 8:8

The Old Testament law outlined very specific guidelines about food: what people could eat, when they could eat it, and how they were to prepare it. There were celebratory and sacred restrictions on food as well as precise directions for preparing and presenting offerings. One was required to abide by these rules and regulations to avoid the appearance of being unclean. Jesus came as fulfillment of the law, and He is not concerned so much with the details of exactly what we eat and drink. It is the studying of God's word and our subsequent obedience to His call that draws us nearer to Him. We are to live our lives based upon the example that Christ set, and we are to encourage those around us to do the same.

The sacrifice of food while you fast is not to deprive you of what you want but to focus you on what, or Whom, you truly need – Jesus. Have you noticed that each day you dine with the Lord, you grow to know Him more intimately? Have you found a peaceful place to retreat while others are eating? My favorite quiet times are in my bedroom because the walls are painted blue, and my bed is white like a cloud. I feel like I'm sitting in the heavens with my Lord! It is good to find a place where you can go to be alone with Him, but, remember that God can be found everywhere. The important thing is not where God is found but just that He is found. Be diligent about seeking Him.

Praise God for your private time alone with Him and for the eternal food with which He fills you.

_____
_____
_____
_____
_____
_____
_____
_____
_____
_____

Dinner

"…'I am the Bread of Life. He who comes to Me will never go hungry,
and he who believes in Me will never be thirsty.' "
– John 6:35

⚜ **Daily Bread** – Read: John 15:5

To be of use to the Lord, we must daily commit ourselves to Him by searching and reading the Scriptures and by confessing and communicating with Him. It's been said that you can't lead others where you haven't been yourself, and we certainly can't offer godly counsel to others if we aren't seeking His counsel for ourselves. We must draw our strength and wisdom from Him. Our eyes should focus not on our problems but on our Savior, because He holds the solutions.

Hold Fast ⚜ 27

When we choose to plant ourselves in His presence, we have no need for fear or worry. He becomes the source of our strength, and our perspective changes. We no longer see our problems as worldly inconveniences but, instead, as productive pruning opportunities. We can do nothing apart from Him, and there is nothing we should want to do without Him.

No portion of physical bread can ever energize us like the strength and power we receive from His spiritual bread. Living and remaining in Him is beyond important; it is vital, because He is the source of our very lives. By rooting ourselves in His care, He becomes our spiritual sustenance; He empowers us, rejuvenates us, and fuels us to bear fruit which, in turn, becomes a power source for others.

As you settle into your quiet time with the Lord, are you discovering a strength that you never before experienced from a physical meal? Are you bearing fruit? Have you had opportunities to share your bounty with others since you've submitted to the care of the Master Gardener?

Reflect on your newly found hardiness, and journal the ways you have seen Him strengthen others whom you've encountered today.

DAY 6

Hold Out for Joy

Breakfast

"Those who sow in tears will reap with songs of joy."
(Psalm 126:5)

⚜ **Daily Bread** – Read: Psalm 121:1-2

As we progress through this fast, it is easy to believe that the journey is all about us. We think that the pain we're suffering and the sacrifice we're making entitles us to some special attention. If everyone only knew what we're enduring! But, this journey is not what we're doing – it's about what God is doing in us and what He will do through us. It's a journey of revelation, and through it, we are becoming more aware – aware of time we waste, aware of opportunities we miss, and aware of gifts we squander. We also are seeing, with renewed vision, those around us who are deeply hurting.

I have a friend who is suffering in tremendous physical pain. Now, I chose this fasting journey, and I can quit at any time. Whenever my discomfort becomes too much to bear, I can abandon ship and dive into a double cheeseburger. But, my friend doesn't have that option. A juicy burger, a chocolate chip cookie, or a hot fudge sundae won't cure her symptoms. She lives in real pain from a real disease with no real answers. I do my best to pray for her daily, and I try my best to encourage her with God's Word, but her journey has been long and arduous. Her wait for an answer seems unbearable – maybe more so than the pain itself. She can't see the light at the end of the tunnel. I see it for her, though. I know from diligently reading Scripture that our God is a God who cares for us, who will never leave us, who loves us, and who heals us. His remedies often require time, and our prescription is to have faith in Him to do what He says He will do, in His perfect timing.

"Much of my prayer time this week has been for my friend and the medical tests she has coming up. Thirty-four more days seems like a long time for this fast, but I know there is an end. I pray for both of us to see clearly that God is at work…to see how He is preparing us, refining us, breaking us, caring for us, sustaining us, and holding us close." (My Fasting Journal, Day 6).

Today, be in prayer for a friend, family member, co-worker, or neighbor who is in physical pain or who is enduring a painful trial. Pray that the people God lays on your heart may know that He is holding them, and pray that they may trust Him for the duration of their personal journey, no matter how long it may be.

_____
_____
_____

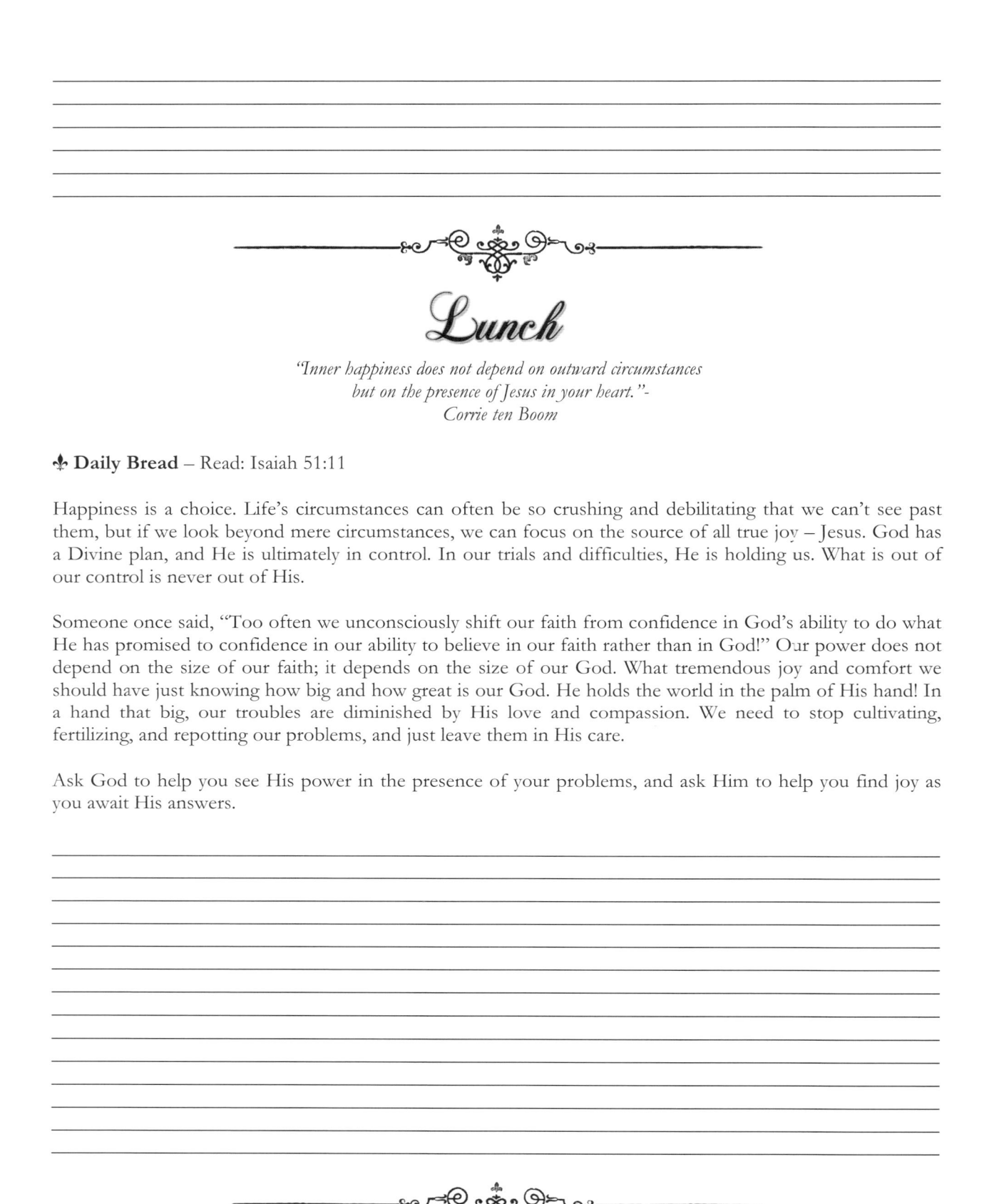

Lunch

"Inner happiness does not depend on outward circumstances but on the presence of Jesus in your heart."-
Corrie ten Boom

⚜ **Daily Bread** – Read: Isaiah 51:11

Happiness is a choice. Life's circumstances can often be so crushing and debilitating that we can't see past them, but if we look beyond mere circumstances, we can focus on the source of all true joy – Jesus. God has a Divine plan, and He is ultimately in control. In our trials and difficulties, He is holding us. What is out of our control is never out of His.

Someone once said, "Too often we unconsciously shift our faith from confidence in God's ability to do what He has promised to confidence in our ability to believe in our faith rather than in God!" Our power does not depend on the size of our faith; it depends on the size of our God. What tremendous joy and comfort we should have just knowing how big and how great is our God. He holds the world in the palm of His hand! In a hand that big, our troubles are diminished by His love and compassion. We need to stop cultivating, fertilizing, and repotting our problems, and just leave them in His care.

Ask God to help you see His power in the presence of your problems, and ask Him to help you find joy as you await His answers.

Dinner

"...'Go and enjoy choice food and sweet drinks and send some to those who have nothing... for the joy of the LORD is your strength.'"
(Nehemiah 8:10)

⚜ **Daily Bread** – Read: Psalm 100

Think back to a time when you had a serious illness, when you went through a difficult trial, when you suffered under a heavy burden, or when you dealt with a difficult person or a difficult situation. Were your immediate thoughts of God and His care? Or, did the full weight of the load you were bearing cause you to lose focus, to worry, and to search for your own solutions rather than turning to the Lord for help?

It is so easy to be held captive in this world and to have your vision limited within the borders of your present circumstances, but God desires that you see your life from His perspective. There is nothing you are enduring that He Himself did not already suffer. He knows your pain, and He knows how much you can bear. He will not let you be crushed by the weight of your difficulties; in fact, He wants you to drop the entire load at His feet because you were never meant to carry it in the first place. Through your adversities, His desire is for you to acknowledge Him as God. Find joy in His strength, and thank Him that you are His child!

Pray for those whom you know do not have a personal relationship with the Lord. Consider the burdens they are unnecessarily bearing alone when they could – and should – release them to Jesus. Ask God to give you the courage to share with them the Source of your strength.

DAY 7
Noise!

Breakfast

"...'Do not be afraid; keep on speaking, do not be silent. For I am with you, and no one is going to attack and harm you . . .'"
(Acts 18:9-10)

✦ **Daily Bread** – Read: Philippians 2:14-15

Did you wake up today to the sound of your stomach grumbling? All that noise sounds like a distress signal. It is an SOS demanding that you put out the fire in your belly – ASAP!

We can become very annoyed at the grumblings of people around us, and, most of the time, we ignore them, but we sometimes let their complaints and lamentations wreak havoc in our day. When your stomach begins to growl today, and it protests that you haven't fed it, stop and enjoy a portion of God's Word. Search the Scriptures for verses on "grumbling" and "complaining". Find some encouragement from Him that you can share the next time you encounter a grumbler. You can fill the empty pit in your stomach with nourishment from God's Holy Word, and you can pull others out of the pit they're in by sharing with them your source of Light and Truth.

During this fast, you are learning to become proactive, rather than reactive, in dealing with the negative and noisy distractions that oppose you throughout the day. Has God alerted you to the things in your life about which you grumble and complain? Do you know someone who exhibits a negative attitude? Can you think of someone who would be characterized as a whiner or a complainer? Offer them some positive and encouraging words; pray that you – and they – may find many more reasons to praise than to protest.

_____
_____
_____
_____
_____
_____
_____
_____

Lunch

*"If I speak in the tongues of men and of angels, but have not love,
I am only a resounding gong or a clanging cymbal."
(1 Corinthians 13:1)*

⚜ **Daily Bread** – Read: 2 Corinthians 4:7-12

"One of the ladies in my Bible study group was sharing today about a woman, in another group she is involved in, who has been so cruel and negative. As a result, this friend of mine has become so discouraged by this lady's accusations that she wants to avoid coming in contact with her. She was in tears over the persecution she is experiencing because of this negative person. We all did our best to encourage her. I tried to explain to her that the Lord was using her as a light in this other group. When people are confronted with light and truth, it exposes a lot of the pain and garbage in their lives. When people are exposed for who they are, they become defensive and lash out, and, typically, they try to take down the one who most represents what they are not. I encouraged her to stand firm and put on the full armor of Christ (Ephesians 6) and to walk into her meetings in peace. The enemy wants her to feel defeated and to run from this opposing force. But, God has put her in this place to be a source of light in this person's life. We never know, but, if it is true that out of the overflow of the heart the mouth speaks (Matthew 12:34b), then this person's heart must be truly hurting. I gave her 2 Corinthians 4:7-12 to meditate on. Lord, allow my friend to be a willing vessel to be used of You to do Your work in this negative person's life. Help her to remain faithful and to have courage to stand against the criticism and the cruelty, and guide her to speak the truth in love. Amen." (My Fasting Journal, Day 7).

The enemy will use people in your life in an attempt to render you useless, hoping that you will turn and run in the opposite direction. When you encounter these people, pray that you will not echo criticism and cruelty, but that you will instead reflect Christ's love. You may be the only person transmitting the love of Jesus to someone else. Pray that the enemy's traps, designed to trip you up, will not cause you to fall, and pray that you may stand firm in Christ's Truth.

Is there someone in your life who is a voice of discouragement? Is there anyone who persecutes you? Ask the Lord to soften this person's heart and to prepare them to receive the light and love that you will radiate in the face of their harassment. Pray for God's strength to help you stand firm. Be diligent about studying the Scriptures for encouragement to help you persevere. A good verse to memorize is Joshua 1:9.

_____
_____
_____
_____
_____
_____
_____
_____
_____
_____
_____
_____
_____
_____
_____

Dinner

"...make the most of every opportunity." – Colossians 4:5

⚜ **Daily Bread** – Read: Colossians 4:2-6

Whether you are fasting for seven days or for 40, you are at end of one week, and the enemy has surely employed a few tactics in a convincing effort to stop you from this seemingly foolish pursuit. His greatest maneuvers trick your mind with discouragement and distraction. It is a daily essential practice to put on the armor of God and the disposition of Christ so that you can rebuke the enemy's deceptive voice with the Word of Truth. The importance of spending time with God can not be overemphasized. Make the most of every opportunity to commune with Him and to talk with Him, as Father and as Friend, so that you will learn to recognize His voice. God does not condemn, confuse, discourage, or destroy – that comes straight from the enemy. The Lord's voice is gentle, compassionate, uplifting, encouraging, and healing.

Take a moment to thank God for all the ways He revealed Himself to you this week, for the strength He gave you, and for the words of encouragement He shared. Praise Him that the noise designed to distract you was silenced by His powerful voice during your quiet time with Him.

2
Stripping Leaves and Growing Roots

" 'Remain in Me, and I will remain in you. No branch can bear fruit by itself; it must remain in the vine. Neither can you bear fruit unless you remain in Me.' "
(John 15:4)

One of my great discoveries through fasting was that I gained so much more than I gave up. My body ached and weakened, but my heart and mind flourished. A wonderful transformation took place inside me, but it didn't happen without necessary work on my part. I had to acknowledge God on a daily basis and believe that He would see me through my journey. I had to devour my Bible instead of my food. I had to talk to God, praying and praising Him throughout each day. And, truly, after each meal with Him, I found that I had the fuel to face whatever came my way. My discernment sharpened; I could judge the Divine opportunities from the enemy distractions. With the Lord as my priority, my time seemed to multiply. Although, or maybe because, I was devoting so much time to God, I managed to accomplish the many tasks on my to-do list in record time!

Something else began to happen, too. As my mind and heart filled with spiritual food, my body emptied in a cleansing process. While I experienced the discomfort of physical waste being expelled from my body, I was also purified of many mental, social, and spiritual wastes. I found many pollutants in my life that were not aligned with God's Truth. Voices of discouragement and worry that had held my mind hostage were released and replaced with Holy encouragement and discernment. Ill will, impatience, and anger were purged and replaced with mercy, peace, and grace. My mild desire to spend a few extra minutes with the Lord was uprooted by a raw hunger aching for the next meal with Him. I could not wait to talk with Him and hear what He had to say, but not everything He said was what I wanted to hear.

When our roots grow towards our Heavenly Father, and we turn our faces to the light of His holiness, He begins the pruning process. It's not always pleasant, and it's often painful. Surrendering food is uncomfortable; surrendering habits is, too. Jesus illustrated many of His parables with food analogies and shared many of His meals with others. I think He chose to do that because food is such a basic human need, and it's something to which we all can relate. We're not to eat, though, just for the sake of eating. What we ingest must be nutritious and beneficial to our bodies. Likewise, what we filter through our minds and hearts must also be pure and wholesome.

God knows we've gotten into some pretty bad habits. He sees how little margin is in our lives and how little time we have for others, especially those closest to us. Our families often suffer, because we are so busy. Through this process of fasting, you're returning to a place where mealtime is pleasant, enjoyable, and fulfilling – a place where you enjoy conversing and communing with those whom you love. The more time you spend with your Father, the more you'll desire to share Him with family members. You'll want them to experience what you have encountered in the presence of your Lord. That is what is meant by John 15:2: *"He cuts off every branch in me that bears no fruit, while every branch that does bear fruit, He prunes so that it will be even more fruitful."* The Lord is to be shared with others! He desires you to become *"like a tree planted by streams of water"*

(Psalm 1:3), so that you will be firmly rooted in Him and so that everyone around you will want to know the Source of your strength and peace.

The process of stripping and pruning is distressing and humbling, but recognizing that God is eliminating your weeds and deepening your roots will make the refinement bearable. He may need to cut you back in order to grow you up. Remain steadfast in Him.

DAY 8

Flip the Switch

Breakfast

"We know from experience that the light of Jesus is stronger than the deepest darkness."
— Betsy ten Boom

⚜ **Daily Bread** – Read: Acts 9:1-19

"Today we had a big snow storm, and we awoke to no electricity. We were not expecting this storm, and we were certainly not expecting to wake up to a cold house. Since it was morning, we were not affected by having no lights. But, we were definitely affected by having no heat. We gathered the kids, and their pillows and blankets, and snuggled around the fireplace, very thankful we had a wood-burning fireplace and a big pile of wood. Church was cancelled because of the snow and ice on the roads. So, this Sunday morning, we enjoyed the fire and basked in the glow of being together as a family." (My Fasting Journal, Day 8).

It's interesting that a force of nature, an act of God, prompts us to simplify our lives. Distractions of television, CD players, video games, and computers fall away, and busy schedules come to a grinding halt as families gather together. No one could penetrate our little bubble that day, and there was definitely no way of escape. The kids, of course, were thrilled at our living room camping excursion. They snuggled up in their sleeping bags, practically one on top of another, as they soaked in the heat of the fire. Our world shrunk to a few square feet, and we all felt safe as we huddled near the hearth. The kid's faces were beaming! They didn't need their fancy electronic gadgets, or any other distracting activity, to make them happy. They were delighted that all of us were together in one place at one time.

It makes me smile to remember it, and I wonder if God smiles when He thinks about the day when all His children will be home, gathered around the warmth of His love, happy to be together, safe within His arms. For a moment on that snowy day, we caught a glimpse of what Heaven will be like.

Sometimes, God powers off the electrical lights in order to reveal His spiritual Light in our hearts and minds. He reminds us that this busy, crazy, meaningless schedule we're keeping is not how He intended us to live. We don't have to make life so complicated! He did not intend for our lives to be filled with so much noise, distraction, and disengagement. He designed us to be content with each other and with Him. He longs for us to interconnect instead of avoiding one another. Occasionally, it takes a flip-of-the-switch to refocus our eyes on what – and Who – is truly important.

Do you recall a time when God flipped the switch for you? Did you receive greater clarity as He enabled you to see things from His perspective? Did you recognize how fruitless your busyness had become?

_____
_____
_____
_____
_____
_____

When was the last time you shut off the world and simply came together with your family?

_____
_____
_____
_____
_____
_____
_____
_____
_____
_____

Lunch

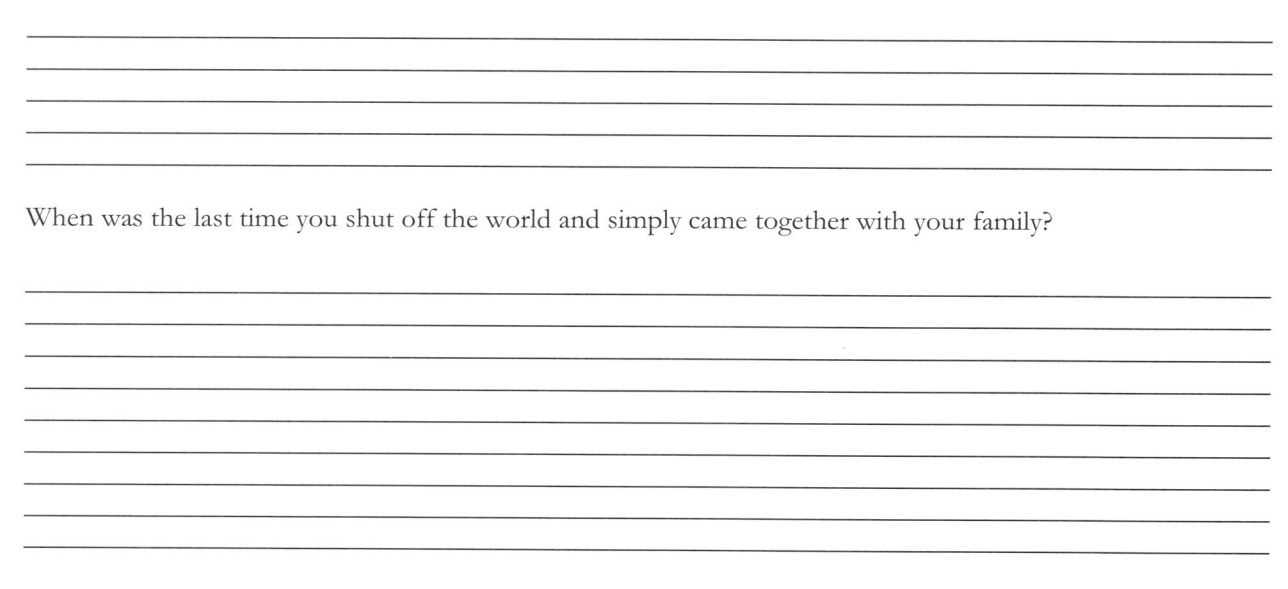

"Your Word is a lamp to my feet and a light for my path."
— Psalm 119:105

⚜ **Daily Bread** — Read: Matthew 4:1-11

"My husband and I had been planning an overnight getaway for the past week, and, when we woke up to a snow-covered yard and an ice-cold house, my first thought was 'This is not what we planned for today!'. We had babysitters scheduled, but the road conditions prevented them from traveling. We had hotel reservations, but we were unable to use them. We had been looking forward to some time alone with each other, but the giggles and laughter in the living room reminded us that we were definitely not alone. Soon, though, I began to wonder why I wanted to leave in the first place; I was so thankful for this moment." (My Fasting Journal, Day 8).

When plans change without notice, one can respond either in frustration or concession. At this point, you are a full week into your fast, and the enemy is still in hot pursuit. He is not willing to give up his attempts to make you trip up. You've gained significant ground in your personal devotional time with the Lord, but when things don't go the way you've planned, will you squander the progress you've made?

That snowy morning, I expected a reward in the form of a weekend vacation with my husband. Instead, I awoke to a test. There were two possible responses: I could recognize the sovereign hand of God at work, accepting this change of plans as a blessing and gift from Him, or, I could lose focus and self-control, allowing my emotions free reign to bind me in selfishness and self-pity. Jesus was tempted by the devil when He was fasting, but He remained composed, winning victory by standing on the Word of God.

Is there a circumstance in your life that has altered your best-laid plans? Are you having difficulty distinguishing the Lord's divinity from the enemy's disruption? Proverbs 19:21 says, *"Many are the plans in a man's heart, but it is the LORD'S purpose that prevails."* Go to God in prayer, and ask Him to guard your heart, guide your mind, and govern your emotions; pray for willingness to accept God's perfect Will above your own intentions.

Dinner

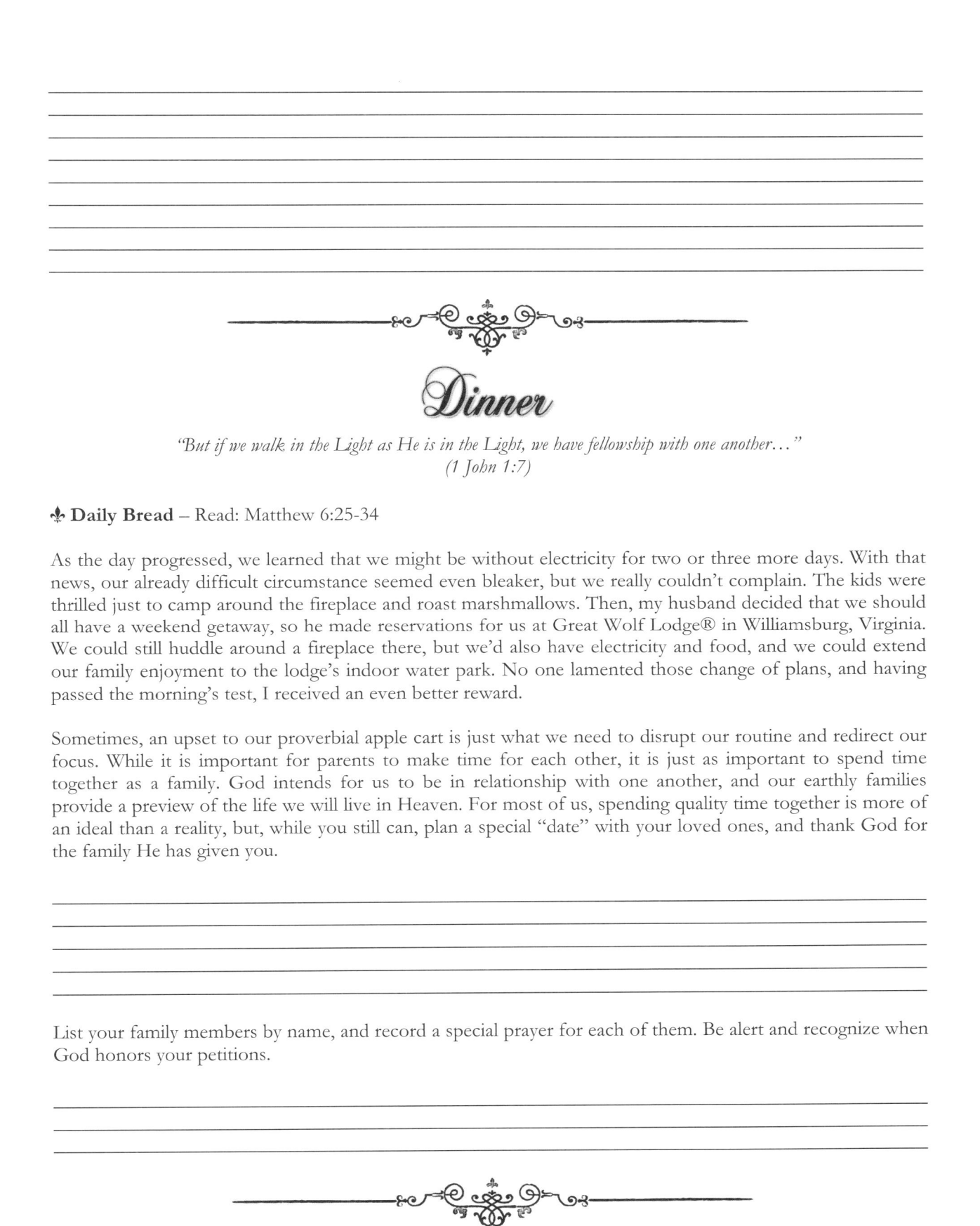

"But if we walk in the Light as He is in the Light, we have fellowship with one another…"
(1 John 1:7)

❧ **Daily Bread** – Read: Matthew 6:25-34

As the day progressed, we learned that we might be without electricity for two or three more days. With that news, our already difficult circumstance seemed even bleaker, but we really couldn't complain. The kids were thrilled just to camp around the fireplace and roast marshmallows. Then, my husband decided that we should all have a weekend getaway, so he made reservations for us at Great Wolf Lodge® in Williamsburg, Virginia. We could still huddle around a fireplace there, but we'd also have electricity and food, and we could extend our family enjoyment to the lodge's indoor water park. No one lamented those change of plans, and having passed the morning's test, I received an even better reward.

Sometimes, an upset to our proverbial apple cart is just what we need to disrupt our routine and redirect our focus. While it is important for parents to make time for each other, it is just as important to spend time together as a family. God intends for us to be in relationship with one another, and our earthly families provide a preview of the life we will live in Heaven. For most of us, spending quality time together is more of an ideal than a reality, but, while you still can, plan a special "date" with your loved ones, and thank God for the family He has given you.

List your family members by name, and record a special prayer for each of them. Be alert and recognize when God honors your petitions.

DAY 9

Wake-up Call

Breakfast

"Therefore, prepare your minds for action; be self-controlled; set your hope fully on the grace to be given you when Jesus Christ is revealed."
(1 Peter 1:13)

✣ **Daily Bread** – Read: Jeremiah 33:3

"How grateful I am for the time away with my family and for the fun we are having! Sitting in the hot tub at the water park has been very relaxing and soothing. Even with this wonderful gift, I've found myself short on temper. Then, I realized I haven't been spending my mealtimes with the Lord. I've spent a lot of time playing with my children and enjoying our time together as a family, but I've been giving so much out and taking so little in." (My Fasting Journal, Day 9).

In retrospect, it's amazing how, in such a short span of time, my emotions returned to rule me. All the time I had spent in the Scriptures and in communion with the Lord that previous week did not build a reserve strong enough to last through a brief vacation. We all need the Lord daily –not just once a day but several times a day, just like eating food. What we eat with the Lord at dinner will not sustain us through the next day. We must habitually and consistently stay in the Word – every day and every meal.

Have you found yourself missing meals with the Lord during your fast? Has the day been so full of activity, that your surrendered time, meant to refuel you with the spirit of God's Word, was misused to squeeze in one more errand or chore? Don't even think about skipping breakfast this morning, no matter how much you "have" to do! How will you ever withstand the grumbling in your belly and the grumblings of people around you if you walk out of that door empty?

This morning, before you do anything else, put on your full armor. Read Ephesians 6:13-18.

_____
_____
_____
_____
_____
_____

Lunch

*"Therefore I tell you, whatever you ask for in prayer,
believe that you have received it, and it will be yours."*
— Mark 11:24

⚜ **Daily Bread** – Read: Matthew 7:7-12

I wonder if the Lord ever gets tired of hearing His children's voices. All day long, I hear "Mommy this" and "Mommy that", "I want this" and "I want that". Sometimes I feel like a short-order cook serving up special requests or a vending machine mechanically distributing individual selections on demand.

I remember the first time I heard the word "Mommy" uttered from my precious baby's lips. I thought my heart would burst from such a beautiful sound, yet that same sound, now sometimes coming from three different mouths at once, is too much of a good thing! I have thought about changing my name to one that I don't hear as often – "Daddy".

Maybe the Lord doesn't tire of hearing His children's voices because they rarely call on Him. And, perhaps, when they do, it's mostly to air laundry list of complaints and problems or to itemize a catalog of demands. We thoughtlessly petition Him with wearisome requests, yet we are seldom willing to do what He asks of us.

I once read that out of all God's Divine assignments, obedience in prayer is the least exercised. What are the strengths and weaknesses in your prayer life? Ask Him what He desires from you and be willing to serve as His hands and feet.

Dinner

"Give thanks to the LORD, call on His name."
(1 Chronicles 16:8a)

⚜ **Daily Bread** – Read: 1 Chronicles 16:8-12

Praising the Lord is the rarest way that we call upon Him. We have so much to ask and so many appeals to present that we frequently neglect to offer Him our thankfulness and gratitude. Our children could receive no better lesson than to see their parents openly and earnestly thanking God for His provision and grace.

We desire and expect that our sons and daughters show a little gratitude and appreciation for what we do for them and for what we give them. Why would our Heavenly Father not require the same from us? Even when our children don't express thanks, we continue to provide for all of their needs and for many of their wants. But, when they unabashedly show their love and thankfulness without other thought or motive, don't we want to do even more for them?

We ask so much from God and often wonder why He seems slow to answer. Perhaps the stalemate stems from our end. I think all of our prayers should begin with hearts of gratitude and voices of praise.

Consider all the ways the Lord has blessed you, and express your thankfulness to Him. Praise Him, too, for the circumstances in your life that you just don't understand, and trust Him to answer your call in unimaginable and extraordinary ways.

DAY 10
Love Bears All

Breakfast

*"But God demonstrates His own love for us in this:
While we were still sinners, Christ died for us."*
(Romans 5:8)

🪻 **Daily Bread** – Read: 1 Corinthians 13

"Today is Valentine's Day – a day to celebrate love and those whom you love. You have blessed us so much, Lord, and I pray that we can always be a great example of Your love to each other and to others in this world. Thank you for Your amazing love; when all others seem to fail, Your love never fails!" (My Fasting Journal, Day 10).

It is truly extraordinary that we don't need to do a single thing to experience the great love of God. We can fail Him a thousand times over, but the depth and breadth of His love for us is immutable. Our human love comes with strings attached; we often require a lot from those around us before extending even a little of our love to them. God's love, however, is unconditional and unchangeable. It always is, always was, and always will be. In a world that constantly shifts and transforms, isn't it comforting to have the consistency of God's love?

I've read before that if you substitute God's name for the word "love" when you read the 13th chapter of 1 Corinthians, you will see a much clearer picture of the kind of love God represents to us and desires for us. You will also discern that agape love is impossible apart from God – the two are inseparable.

There are many emotions surfacing as you press on through the second week of your fast, and you may feel as though you will fail. Do not give up! Cling to the One whose love never fails, and ask Him for an extra helping of it this week.

This morning, express your gratitude to God for His amazing love for you, and thank Him for the many people He has brought into your life whom you love and who love you. Pray for those who are less than loving and difficult to love, and remember how great God's love is for them. Pray that their hearts are softened as they experience the magnitude of His love today.

_____
_____
_____
_____
_____

Lunch

"(Love) . . . is not easily angered." – 1 Corinthians 13:5c

✠ **Daily Bread** – Read: Luke 15:11-32

In one of my morning devotionals, I was struck by the story of the prodigal son. I've read this story many times before, but the writer of this particular devotional pointed out that this was an extraordinary example of agape love. When the lost son demanded his inheritance, the father didn't reply with angry words about ungrateful children; he held his tongue, and, in calmness, he thought more clearly and chose to react in love.

I thought about the many times that we, in our sinful human natures, get so upset and lose our tempers when people make demands of us when, instead, we should step back and truly comprehend what is being asked and, most importantly, why it is being asked. Recognizing the motive behind the request is very revealing.

Here is a story of a boy demanding everything from a father who has never withheld anything from him, and the father just opens his hands, opens his heart, and gives his son all for which he asks. Why does the man not say "No!", or, at least, tell the boy what a ridiculous request he is making? Why doesn't the father explain to his son how his future will be affected by his impulsive demand? Are we not accountable to inform people of the error of their ways when we see them heading down a path of destruction? Why wouldn't a father who loves his son so much try to stop him from making a huge mistake?

The father's unconditional love for his son is the very reason he doesn't stop him. It's the same reason our heavenly Father doesn't try to stop us when we make hasty, ill-informed, and unwise decisions. When someone tries to convince another to choose differently, the resulting action of the offending party is usually attempted rationalization and justification for the errant decision. This father did the only thing that he could do to express his unconditional love for his son – he let go, and he prayed.

And, because of his father's calm response and loving demeanor, the son did not have a second thought when he was ready to come home. He knew that he had wasted his life, and he knew that he had disappointed his father, but he also knew that the last time he saw his father's face, it was full of love. The son could only hope that the same love, which willingly let him depart a spoiled brat, would welcome him home as a humble slave.

When the son finally did return home, he found his father just as he had left him – with open arms and a loving heart. It makes absolutely no sense to us when someone chooses a path fraught with danger and destined for destruction, but we must learn from the parable of the prodigal son's father and from the example of our Heavenly Father. We must be willing to accept those whom we love – just as they are – and to forgive them when do finally realize the error of their ways. We must let them come home to someone who loves them!

Our Lord's love remains undisturbed no matter how ridiculously we behave; His awesome love always prevails. To what part of the prodigal son story do you most relate? I think, at some time or another, we've all walked in the shoes of both the father and the son. Ask the Lord for strength, wisdom, and self-control to lessen your childish rebelliousness, and pray that you may always personify His unconditional love.

Dinner

"My son, do not despise the LORD's discipline and do not resent His rebuke, because the Lord disciplines those He love…"
– Proverbs 3:11-12

⚜ **Daily Bread** – Read: John 15:1-2

I read a fasting journal in which the author likened her journey to the tree in her front yard that was 'stark and vulnerable without leaves or blossoms'. She, too, felt stripped and emptied. I can relate to her metaphor, and we are all susceptible to the Lord's careful pruning. He is the vine, and we are the branches, and it's not until we are truly gutted of worldly distractions and material desires that we can bear God's intended fruit.

"I truly understand during this fast that I need to be totally dependent on You, Lord, each day. Like a branch without a tree, I am lifeless and useless without You, but, if I remain in You and trust You to do Your work in my life, I will become useful for You. If I don't start each day in the Word, and if I don't abide in You moment by moment, my emotions get the best of me. Teach me to do nothing out of my own energy – I have so little of it anyway. Let me abide constantly in You. Amen." (My Fasting Journal, Day 10).

Day 10 is coming to a close. Find time to reflect on this day and this week. What is the Lord bringing to your attention? Where is He pruning you? Rest in Him and trust Him during the process. You may appear weak and frail, but God is making you fruitful and beautiful.

DAY 11
Bearing One Another's Burdens

Breakfast

"Carry each other's burdens, and in this way you will fulfill the law of Christ."
(Galatians 6:2)

⚜ **Daily Bread** – Read: Romans 15:1-6

During this fast, you may become consumed with your own weakness, difficulty, and lethargy. You may hardly be able to think of anyone except yourself. However, the discipline of denying yourself actually enhances your sensitivity to the needs of others and increases your awareness of God's power in your life.

Romans 15:1 exhorts, *"We who are strong ought to bear with the failings of the weak and not to please ourselves."* It's difficult to imagine that you are strong when you feel so weak, but, as you're fasting, you're learning to gain your strength from the most stable source – your Heavenly Father. Depending on Him for energy and fulfillment will sustain you far beyond mere physical food.

Just as you normally set aside time to eat three meals a day (not including snacks!), it is important that you come to His table regularly throughout the day. Some people need to eat more frequently than others and in smaller portions. The same may be true of your need to dine with the Lord. The awesome wonder of His table is that it is always prepared, and He is always waiting for you. His bounty is endless, and you can come as often as you like!

Do not deceive yourself by believing that you can skip meals and still build up the energy and nutrition you need to sustain a healthy existence. You will not be strong enough to resist temptations if you miss your square meals. An unhealthy snack can give you a quick fix, yet it provides no lasting sustenance and no nutritional value; it ruins your appetite for nourishing food while polluting your body with empty calories. Likewise, starving your spirit with counterfeit cuisine – spiritual "fast food", if you will – wreaks the same kind havoc.

When you regularly dine with the Lord, your strength will become obvious, and people will be curious about the source. If you have been eating wisely, you will be able to speak the wholesome Truth from God's Word. If you've been skipping meals and sneaking shortcuts, you will have only your own unsound opinions to offer.

It is no small matter that the Lord brings certain people into your life and entrusts them to your care. Take seriously the responsibility of sharing His truth, and prepare sufficiently. When people need help, only God's wisdom will suffice.

Pray that the Lord will make you more aware of the people He is planting in your path, and ask Him to speak through you so that they will receive nothing but what He intends for them: the Truth, the whole Truth and nothing but the Truth.

___

Lunch

"Praise be to the Lord, to God our Savior, who daily bears our burdens."
(Psalm 68:19)

⚜ **Daily Bread** – Read: Ephesians 4:2

As I've mentioned, I have a friend who is suffering with a terrible, chronic pain, and the doctors can not find its source. Little can comfort my friend, and no one can help her. I know that the Lord called me to "stand in the gap" for her, so I am praying for her. She has so little strength, and she's stalled at a very difficult place in her journey. It has been a long one with no answers, and, now, she is losing hope. I don't even know how to help her; the words I offer do little to encourage her because she is questioning God, and talking about her pain is the last things she wants to do because she just wants it gone.

Praying on her behalf one day, the Lord led me to the story in the 17th chapter of Matthew about the boy possessed by an evil spirit; his father was desperately seeking healing for him. The disciples could not heal him, only Jesus could, and He told them, *". . . this kind goeth not out but by prayer and fasting."* (Matthew 17:21 KJV).

Nothing can rival the power of a desperate child of God who humbly and earnestly submits to Him in prayer. No one has the power to do what God can do through the fervent prayers of a believer who is out of other options. God's help and healing, sought by the prayer and fasting of His children, is illustrated throughout Scripture (see Ezra 8:23, Esther 4:16, 1 Samuel 7:6).

That power is available to us, too, when we fast and pray on behalf of our family, our friends, our country, and our world. Tap into the ultimate Power; pray for those who want fiercely to be healed, and pray for those who are unaware that they need to be. The world teems with suffering and hurting people, and many of them do not even have the strength – or the knowledge – to get on their knees. Ask God to show you how to intercede for them.

_____
_____
_____
_____
_____
_____
_____
_____
_____
_____

Dinner

". . . My yoke is easy and My burden is light." – Matthew 11:30

⚜ **Daily Bread** – Read: Matthew 11:28-30

Our fast-paced culture discourages us from actually stopping, tuning in to those around us, and really listening to their needs. Praying for them and searching the Scriptures on their behalf is next to impossible, given our jam-packed, no-margin schedules.

Jesus, more than anyone, knew about a hectic and demanding life. Throngs of people followed Him, clung to Him, grabbed at Him, questioned Him, but He never failed to seek solitude with His Father for communion, prayer, and guidance. Jesus set an important example; He knew that time with the Father was the only way to experience true rest.

Burdens are set aside only when we release them into the hands of our loving Father. No matter how hard we try, no matter how good our intentions may be, no matter how strong we think we are, we simply do not have the power to carry our own burdens, let alone the burdens of others. We can really get ourselves into trouble if, in our attempts to help someone in need, we rely only on our own limited strength and knowledge. Family, friends, and co-workers can become very dependent, especially if they perceive us as having the answers to their problems, and we can quickly grow weary from bearing their burdens. But, we're not meant to bear their burdens, and, we're cheating the very person we're attempting to help if we do not represent Christ as the source of all power.

It's only when people turn to Jesus that they learn to tap into the true source of all strength and wisdom. Our own power is in limited supply and in constant need of God's renewal. Our job requires us not to take on the burdens of another but, rather, to offer them the Word of God, to pray with them, and to direct them to the Divine power source.

The old Chinese proverb teaches, *"If you give a man a fish, you feed him for a day; but, if you teach a man to fish, you feed him for a lifetime."* Teaching and training usually require more initial effort on our part, but the payoff yields a child of God who relies solely on the Heavenly Father.

Pray that God would show you how to go the distance with those who desire to know the Source of your strength, and remember that you will always be a student yourself. There is so much to learn, and Jesus is our patient Teacher.

DAY 12

Finding Water

Breakfast

"He is like a tree planted by streams of water..."
(Psalm 1:3a)

⚜ **Daily Bread** – Read: Isaiah 58:11

This time of fasting may seem like time in the desert. You feel weak, dry, and lonely, but you are not alone. You are, in fact, right where God wants you to be. You are daily reading His Word, seeking His face, talking to Him, and communing with Him. This encounter is no mirage in a dry desert wasteland; it is an oasis in a parched and darkened world. You are experiencing a very real and awesome privilege – a Holy and Divine invitation to sit at a beautifully adorned banqueting table, to lounge in the lap of your loving Savior, to soak in the rays of His glorious light, and to taste His sweet Word like honey on your tongue.

The enemy wishes for you to feel isolated and alone, but you are actually engulfed in your Savior's gracious adoration as He tenderly sustains and cares for you. Just as a plant finds water by rooting far below the surface of the earth, the deeper you root yourself in Christ, the better His Spirit will hydrate you. Dig deep into the well of the Scriptures, and do not become discouraged when you encounter enemy obstructions designed to impede your progress. Do not abandon your diligent search for Truth; God's reservoir is deep and wide!

As you drink your breakfast this morning, think about what God has revealed to you so far during your pilgrimage. You are nearing the end of your second week with Him. While there are many more days ahead, be encouraged by what you've been shown and how much you've grown.

Your roots are growing deep. Let the Lord refresh you, fill you, and prepare you for the day ahead. Commit to staying firmly planted in Him, and look forward to the next stage of your development.

_____
_____
_____
_____

Lunch

*"I will sprinkle clean water on you, and you will be clean;
I will cleanse you from all your impurities . . ."*
(Ezekiel 36:25)

⚜ **Daily Bread** – Read: John 4:14

I drank a lot of water during my fast, but, each evening, I would enjoy a small cup of orange-pineapple juice. Even though much of the published information about fasting recommends avoiding citrus juice, I found a little cupful to be very refreshing. It's time now to pour your favorite afternoon beverage, pull up a chair, and enjoy your lunch with the Lord.

I love the special lunches that I occasionally share with a dear friend or with my best friend, my husband. But, today, drink in the knowledge that you are having lunch with the King of Kings! I don't know how that makes you feel, but the very thought of it totally blows my mind.

The Lord constantly amazes me with new insights; sometimes, as I read a Scripture that I have read a dozen times before, it just leaps off the page with fresh meaning. When that happens, God is granting me a new depth of understanding. When we first come to know Him, we graze the surface layers of His Word, but, as we grow and mature, the significance, as well as the application, of those very same Words is greatly enhanced.

When we endure struggles and persevere through trials, we have a more thorough understanding of what other believers have experienced. When we continue to learn through Bible studies, sermon messages, and personal devotions, we can better appreciate the Holy Scriptures. God's Word means more to us because we have a greater desire to learn more about Him. We earnestly want to increase our comprehension of His Word, and He willingly wants to teach us.

I had LASIK surgery on my eyes a couple of years ago after wearing contact lenses and glasses for twenty years. Amazingly, I walked into the laser room seeing only blurred images, but, in less than five minutes, I could see the hands on the clock across the room! My otherwise normal day was brightened with exceptional clarity in just a brief amount of time.

Spending mere minutes with the Lord can also result in life-altering clarity. By meditating on His Truth, reading His Word, and talking with Him, we gain laser-like accuracy and lucidity in our understanding of Him. And, the more time we spend with Him, the clearer our own path will become. Ask the Lord to illuminate your life each day to ensure that your cloudy vision becomes clear and sharp.

Dinner

"Never again will they hunger; never again will they thirst.
The sun will not beat upon them, nor any scorching heat."
(Revelation 7:16)

⚜ **Daily Bread** – Read: John 7:37-38

"Tonight, I went to a birthday party at a friend's house. Usually in the evenings, I am tired, so I was finding it difficult to relax while everyone was eating and enjoying cake and ice cream. But, I knew this was where I needed to be. Later, after all the guests had left, my friend pulled me aside and poured out her aching heart to me." (My Fasting Journal, Day 12).

If we make ourselves available for God's service, no matter how weary we are, He will use us for His greater purposes. He accomplishes His greatest work through us when we are at our weakest. Throughout his writings, Paul evidenced delight in his deficiencies because, through his weakness, Christ's strength was revealed. The credit for what is accomplished through us belongs only to God.

But, we must tap into the Fountain of Life before He will flow through us. We can't expect the sprinkler to water the yard if it's not hooked up to the faucet! As you pray tonight, be refreshed in the Scriptures, and become saturated with His grace and love. Then, make yourself available for God to pour out His mercy on a thirsty friend.

DAY 13
Soaking Wet

Breakfast

". . . In my distress, I called to the LORD, and He answered me." – Jonah 2:2a

⚜ **Daily Bread** – Read: Jonah 2:1-10

When the Lord's Living Water washes over us, it does more than just refresh and revive us; it cleanses us. The story of Jonah is a great illustration of how a good soaking can compel us to confess our unwillingness and get back on track with the Lord.

Jonah decided he wasn't going to obey God, and, in his attempt to circumvent God's plan, he inadvertently boarded a ship filled with pagan sailors – very ironic considering that his argument for avoiding Nineveh hinged on his reluctance to deal with pagan people there! Many of us also run away from what God has called us to do, rationalizing that we know better than He, but we quickly find ourselves in a situation far worse than the one we attempted to sidestep in the first place. Our case study, Jonah, tried to dodge his God-given responsibility to deliver a message to the wicked people of Nineveh only to find himself being literally transported by the very same kind of people he was trying to avoid. And, then, of course, the storm hit.

When storms disrupt your life, you may wonder why. Often, God is trying to get your attention. When the same squall hits you again and again, harder and harder, it's a good indication that God is flushing you out of hiding from behind the perceived protection of your flimsy umbrella. At first, Jonah just flat-out ignored the storm; he didn't even acknowledge it. The funny thing is that the pagans begged Jonah to ask His God to save them. He wouldn't do it, so they did.

Though heathen, those people were very aware and fearful of this powerful God that Jonah worshiped. Jonah himself seemed pretty dispassionate about the entire ordeal, but he knew how to calm the storm because God had already given him the answer with his original marching orders to Nineveh. When the sailors took Jonah's God-given advice and tossed him into the sea, the storm calmed, and there was Jonah, soaking wet in the middle of the ocean. Then, he was rescued – okay, the exact Scripture reference says he was swallowed by a great fish. (Hint: sometimes the vehicle God uses to rescue us is not exactly what we had in mind, but it's exactly what we need to transport and redirect us to God's intended course.)

In the end, God accomplishes His original plan (in spite of Jonah's unnecessary but enlightening decision to travel the scenic route). Jonah eventually did go to Nineveh where he obediently proclaimed God's word to the Ninevites who, in turn, fasted, prayed, and abandoned their wicked ways. Their repentance prompted a Divine response. God had mercy on them and saved them from imminent destruction.

Sometimes, we are a lot like Jonah. We know what we are supposed to do; we even know that it is God-ordained, but we are more fearful of the task itself than of the consequences of our disobedience. Other people shouldn't scare us, but disappointing God should make us shake in our proverbial boots. If He has called us to a Divine task, we have no reason to fear because He has already prepared the hearts of those who are to receive our message.

Instead of running from your fears, pray this morning for the Lord to help you face the source of them, and pray for the courage to travel wherever He leads you. Pray, too, for those who do not have the precious gift that you have already received – the gift of eternal life through the shed blood of Jesus Christ. Pity the unsaved, but do not fear them.

_____
_____
_____
_____
_____
_____
_____
_____
_____
_____

Lunch

". . . my sins are cast into the deepest sea, and God posts a sign that says, 'No Fishing Allowed!'."
– Corrie ten Boom

⚜ **Daily Bread** – Read: Isaiah 59:1-2

As you daily seek God, and as the truth of His Word enters your heart, the available space for things and thoughts that separate you from Him shrinks. He calls you to holiness because He is Holy, and the more you emulate Him, the more perfect your character becomes.

Jonah was a man who heard from God on a regular basis; one would think he was a holy and righteous man without any problems. But, just because he heard from God didn't mean he was living for God. Jonah, like many other believers, was a work in progress.

When Jesus begins His work in us, a lot of cleaning, purging, and scouring takes place. In Jonah's life, that housekeeping was evidenced as he, God's chosen messenger, reverted to a disobedient, willful, rebellious child. But, God loves us too much to allow us to get away with defiant misbehavior. Too much is at stake; eternity hangs in the balance as God trusts us to take His message where He directs us.

After Jonah got a good soaking (i.e. cleansing), God redirected him to Nineveh. This time, as you'll remember, he journeyed there in the belly of a fish. God did not let Jonah off the hook and successfully captured his full attention. Jonah had much to confess; maybe that explains his fear of going to Nineveh. Perhaps the condition of his own heart shamed him, and he believed himself hypocritical to deliver God's message. Our awesome, omniscient God knew the root of Jonah's disobedience, and, in His grace and mercy, He enabled Jonah to surrender, confess, and renew his spirit.

Daily confession enables God to work in our lives. We should pray, as David prayed in Psalm 51:10, *"Create in me a pure heart, O God, and renew a steadfast spirit within me."* The Lord has a plan for our lives that involves reaching the world. In order to be effective on the outside, it is necessary for Him to purify our insides. Unnecessary baggage only hinders us from accomplishing God's will. Surrendering to God, whether from the side of a mountain, the bottom of a pit, or the belly of a whale, allows Him to work in us and through us.

Pray to receive Divine discernment. Record what God reveals, confess it, and cast it deep into the ocean of God's forgiveness.

_____
_____
_____
_____
_____
_____
_____
_____
_____
_____

Dinner

"Forgiveness is not an emotion – it is an act of the will, and the will can function regardless of the temperature of the heart." – Corrie ten Boom

⚜ **Daily Bread** – Read: Colossians 3:13-14

We bask in God's forgiveness, so why do we balk at forgiving others? Jesus died for everyone. It doesn't matter where they go to church, where they live, or what language they speak; God loves them and extends them the same grace and mercy that He offers us.

Fresh from his own life-transforming pardon, Jonah still scorned the compassion and mercy that God granted the Ninevites. Scripture declares he "*became angry*" (Jonah 4:1). An entire nation escaped the wrath of God, and Jonah was just plain peeved. God alone determines who He saves; what right did Jonah have to judge the Lord's Divine grace? His Word asserts, *"He is patient with you, not wanting anyone to perish, but everyone to come to repentance."* (2 Peter 3:9). Is this not the same forgiveness that Jonah experienced first-hand?

God calls us to forgive as we've been forgiven (Luke 6:37c). We're not authorized to question the command. He requires, not suggests, that we forgive each other. We must forgive those who criticize us, deceive us, hurt us, ignore us, judge us, reject us, and yes, even those who refuse to forgive us. Without extending God's mercy to others, we remain hostage to our sin, and God longs to release those chafing chains and free us from our bondage.

The Lord forgives, and so must we. Confess areas of unforgiveness today; ask Him to fill your heart with love and compassion for all people, especially those who are unloving and dispassionate to you. Heal, and be healed!

DAY 14
Firm Foundation

Breakfast

"The ground on which I build my faith is not in me, but in the faithfulness of God."
— Father ten Boom

⚜ **Daily Bread** – Read: Exodus 14:29-31

You've just been soaked to the bone. You may be dripping wet, but God will soon set your feet on solid ground.

It seems that before the Lord sets His followers on dry ground, we must first traverse a watery grave, confessing our sins and receiving His forgiveness. Baptism, an important Christian ordinance, publicly displays a believer's personal decision to accept Christ's death, burial, and resurrection.

We just witnessed Jonah's aquatic cleansing, and now we will behold the Israelites' dusty deliverance. In the Exodus, Moses led the Israelites out of their captivity in Egypt. When they arrived at the edge of sea with the Egyptian army in hot pursuit, fear overwhelmed them. At this stage in their journey, we may agree that their panic resulted from a long captivity that denied them any previous taste of freedom. They accused Moses of leading them to their deaths in the desert, but, had they studied their genealogy, they would have known that the desert is God's favorite meeting place. In a true *"I am the Lord Your God"* fashion, He arrived right on time. Moses comforted the Israelites, *"Do not be afraid. Stand firm, and you will see the deliverance the Lord will bring you today . . . The Lord will fight for you; you need only to be still."* (Exodus 14:13-14).

To remain still when every human instinct screams, "Run!" requires immense faith and total trust in God. God called His promised nation to believe and depend upon Him, and, despite miracle after miracle, the tracks of their faith walk proved slow and unsteady. But, time after time, regardless of the Israelites' response, God was faithful.

On this particular day, standing on the shoreline of the Red Sea, the Israelites experienced a Divine deliverance like no other. At the direction of the Lord, Moses raised his staff and stretched his hand out over the sea; the water divided with a strong east wind, and *"the Israelites went through the sea on dry ground, with a wall of water on their right and on their left."* (Exodus 14:22). That day, as recorded in verse 30a of the same book and chapter, "the LORD saved Israel from the hands of the Egyptians."

As they walked right through the middle of the sea, the Lord's chosen people witnessed the power, protection, and provision of the Most High God. They experienced first-hand the depth and breadth of His great love for them, a love that He continually extends to all of His children, including you and me. That same love culminated with the lifting of another mighty stick, this time in the form of a cross. With the outstretched hands of Jesus covering humankind from east to west, and God tearing the temple curtain in half from top to bottom. This offering and final sacrifice allows all of God's children the opportunity to bridge the great divide and enter His presence. The deliverance of the Israelites was but a preview of the great deliverance to come. Sadly, when He arrived, few were paying attention.

Are you willing to stand as a testimony to His great love? Will you share your own story of liberation with those who desperately and urgently need to hear it? Will you be still, stand firm, and trust in Him when all else seems frightening and unsure?

Record your own song of deliverance, and praise the Lord for His provision.

_____
_____
_____
_____
_____
_____
_____
_____
_____
_____

Lunch

"On Christ, the solid Rock, I stand; all other ground is sinking sand."
— Hymn of Grace by Edward Mote, circa 1834

⚜ **Daily Bread** – Read: Psalm 40:1-3

The Lord plucked the Israelites from the sludge of a seemingly worthless existence and set their feet on solid ground as His chosen people. He marched them through the sea, and, on the other side, they found a new freedom and a fresh confidence in their Great Provider. God protected and sustained them day after day, month after month, year after year. He continues to do the same for His believers today.

God lifts us from our pits, cleansing and restoring us. He sets us on higher ground with higher purposes, and He Himself serves as our Cornerstone. The Lord gives us a new song, and its refrain draws others to Him. He designed us to serve as living testimonies of His great love and of His extreme desire to deliver us from the depths of our despair.

Stand firm, and stay focused on Him. Rest your fear in Him. Be still, and trust in Him. He chose you, and you must choose Him. The world may rise against you, but, even – and especially – at the brink of the impasse, take refuge in this Word from the Lord: *"Do not be afraid or discouraged because of this vast army. For the battle is not yours, but God's. You will not have to fight this battle. Take up your positions; stand firm and see the deliverance the Lord will give you."* (2 Chronicles 20:15b, 17a).

You do not have to fight the battle, but you must dress for it. Review (Do you have it memorized by now?) Ephesians 6:13-17, and suit up.

Dinner

"Listen to Me, you who pursue righteousness and who seek the LORD: Look to the Rock from which you were cut . . ." – Isaiah 51:1

⚜ **Daily Bread** – Read: Matthew 7:24-25

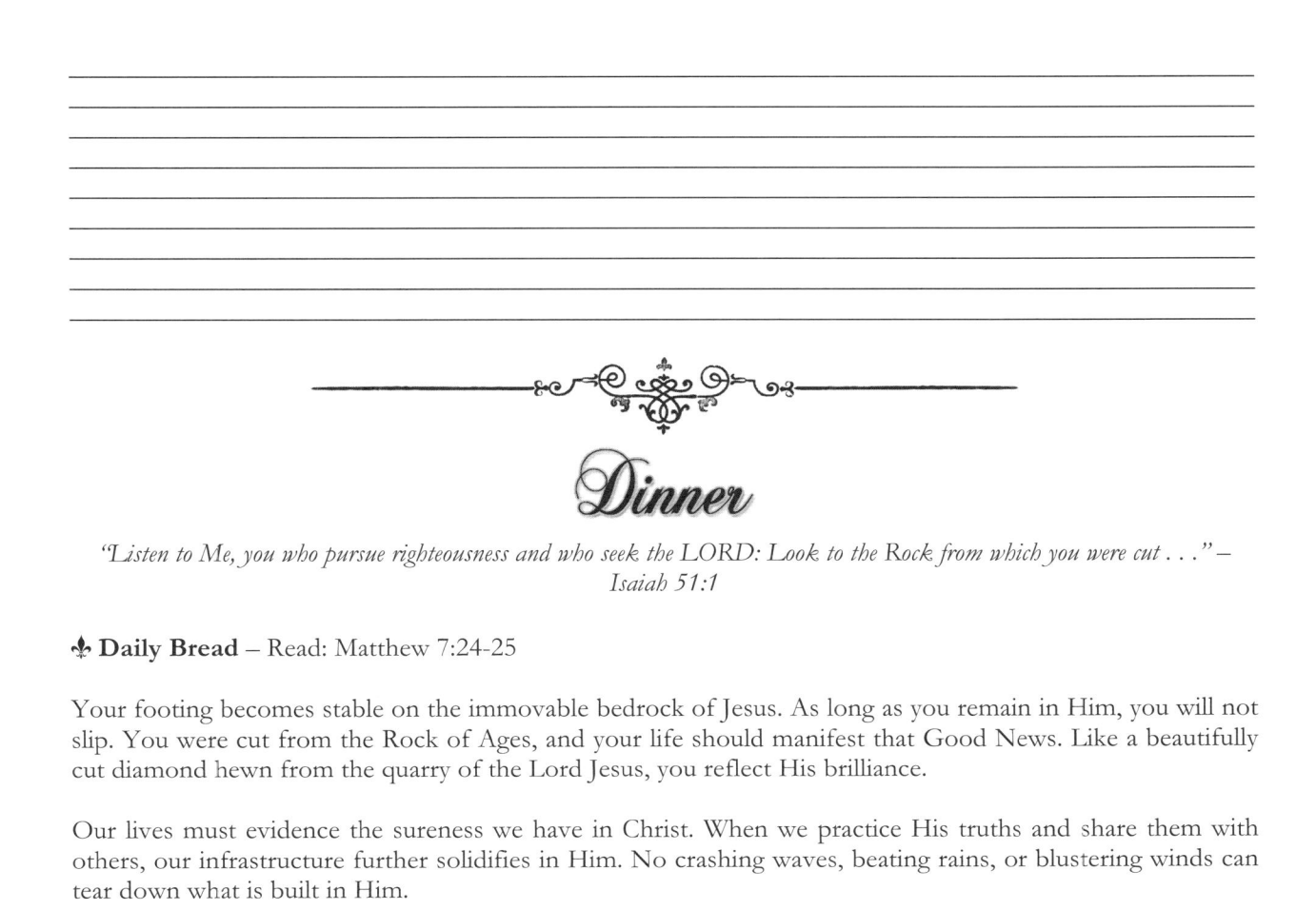

Your footing becomes stable on the immovable bedrock of Jesus. As long as you remain in Him, you will not slip. You were cut from the Rock of Ages, and your life should manifest that Good News. Like a beautifully cut diamond hewn from the quarry of the Lord Jesus, you reflect His brilliance.

Our lives must evidence the sureness we have in Christ. When we practice His truths and share them with others, our infrastructure further solidifies in Him. No crashing waves, beating rains, or blustering winds can tear down what is built in Him.

Be diligent to build a firm foundation in Christ. Lay your groundwork carefully and deliberately, brick by brick, with the mortar of His precious love. Thoughtfully apply each of His principles as you exercise His truths. Every test only fortifies your strength in Christ, as long as you reside within the walls of His Word.

Your pursuit of God's Truth is becoming as natural and as regular as eating. However, you must do more than just digest the Bread of Life. You eat to live, and you must live what you eat by sharing it with others. God's sustenance is limitless. As you fuel yourself, think of others with whom you can share, and break Bread together.

3
Perseverance and Prayer

"…No eye has seen, no ear has heard, no mind has conceived what God has prepared for those who love Him – but God has revealed it to us by His Spirit. The Spirit searches all things, even the deep things of God."
(1 Corinthians 2:9-10)

This week, you reach the midpoint in your 40-day fast. By now, you've developed a good routine, and you've eliminated many distractions. You've also become more attuned to specific areas in your life where God is refining you. As He continues to purge your impurities, they sometimes appear uglier than ever as they surface, but be assured that the process is necessary, and, in the healing transformation, blemishes usually magnify before they minimize and ultimately disappear.

God's sanctifying holiness clarifies your clouded vision, enabling you to see others in His Light. You now begin to view others through the loving eyes of Jesus, and, in your fresh perception, they appear not as time-sucking nuisances but as precious children of the Living God who need our encouragement and His salvation. But, still, you've only scratched the surface. There is far more digging to do. The Lord has more to show you, more than you can even imagine.

A biography of Corrie ten Boom, shares the reassurance that she received from her sister, Betsy, in the ghastly midst of the German concentration camps: "There is no place so deep that God is not deeper still."

Yesterday, today, and tomorrow, we can find Him wherever we go, and there is no place we can go where He has not already been. Before Jesus began his three-year public ministry on earth, He Himself fasted for 40 days and 40 nights. He fasted; He prayed; He faced temptation of the highest degree, yet He remained pure and holy. *"For we do not have a High Priest who is unable to sympathize with our weaknesses, but we have One who has been tempted in every way, just as we are – yet was without sin."* (Hebrews 4:15).

The fourth chapter of Matthew records the temptation of Jesus in the desert. He experienced everything that you are experiencing now. He knows that in your state of hunger and weakness, you are vulnerable to enemy attacks. He was, too, but He used the Sword of the Spirit, the Holy Scriptures, to outsmart the enemy. There is no other way to win against the evil forces in this world. Jesus exemplified that prayer, coupled with a daily diet of God's Word, provides the essential fuel to strengthen and sustain you during an onslaught of enemy aggression. *"For our struggle is not against flesh and blood, but against the rulers, against the authorities, against the powers of this dark world and against the spiritual forces of evil in the heavenly realms."* (Ephesians 6:12).

In the two weeks you've fasted, you've learned much, but I urge you to persevere and press on. There is so much more to come! I did not receive my greatest revelations until the final week of my fast, and, even a month later, the Lord continued to enlighten me.

I believe there is great significance in the fact that Jesus fasted for 40 days prior to commencing His earthly ministry. Your call to fast is no less important. The Lord has a place and a purpose for each of us, and He will not lead us without preparing us for His mission. Trust Him for the great plans He has for you; believe Him for the work He is completing in you; know that He is fortifying and expanding the Body of Christ.

When your individual body is spiritually strong, the rest of the Body (the Church) benefits from your good health. Pray for tenacity, and pray for the fortitude of others who are also fasting. God's wonderful work transforms one life at a time. This week, thank Him that His awesome effort in your life did not end when your salvation began; He faithfully labors in you every day of your life! *". . . He who began a good work in you will carry it on to completion until the day of Christ Jesus."* (Philippians 1:6). Be aware, and continue on towards the prize He set before you.

DAY 15
Refreshment

Breakfast

*"As the deer pants for streams of water, so my soul pants for You, O God.
My soul thirsts for God, for the living God. When can I go and meet with God?"*
(Psalm 42:1-2)

⚜ **Daily Bread** – Read: Psalm 42

Have you ever been truly thirsty…so thirsty that your mouth is parched, and your lips are blistered? I remember going to the emergency room for an illness; the doctor determined that I was dehydrated because even my tear ducts didn't work. I was so ill, so weak, and in such distress, I couldn't even cry.

Romans 8:26 beautifully illustrates God's mediation when we ourselves are wrung dry: *"In the same way, the Spirit helps us in our weakness. We do not know what we ought to pray for, but the Spirit Himself intercedes for us with groans that words cannot express."* When we have nothing left to give, when our tears are drained dry, when we are too weak to even cry out to Him, God, in His infinite wisdom, provides His Spirit to intervene for us. What a glorious example of God's great love for us! He knows our needs; we don't even have to voice them, but He desires that we do. And, when we are too feeble to call on Him, His Holy Spirit picks up where we leave off.

God is always present to give you what you need. He will meet you right where you are. This morning, satisfy your physical thirst with a cup of tea, a glass of juice, or a bottle of water, and ask Him to quench your thirsting spirit. Spend time praising Him and thanking Him for hearing your silent cries.

Are you thirsting for God? How do you need the intercession of His Holy Spirit?

_____
_____
_____
_____
_____
_____
_____
_____

Lunch

"Then we will not turn away from You; revive us, and we will call on Your Name."
(Psalm 80:18)

⚜ **Daily Bread** – Read: Acts 3:19

You can start the day in the Word, on your knees with the Lord, but, as the day progresses, you may quickly find yourself wishing to close the door on the world's intrusions and longing to return – alone – to the peace of His Holy presence. Your time with God early in the morning is vital, but you must also find additional time to meet with Him during the day, or you will quickly find yourself stranded.

Many things can physically refresh you in the middle of the day: a quick nap, a relaxing walk, a nutritious snack, a large Chick-fil-A® sweet tea (okay, that last one is my personal favorite!), but nothing can bolster and invigorate you like time with the Lord.

At this point in my fast, the Lord really proved Himself to be my Sustainer. In the past, I've skipped meals and even fasted a few times in an effort to lose weight, but, in those instances, I relied upon my own determination, and my goal was physical rather than spiritual. When you fast unto the Lord, however, you receive all the benefits of weight loss and you experience greater health, but, most importantly, you gain the peace that comes from surrendering all control to the omnipotence of the Living God. When you are sustained by the awesome power of the Bread of Life, as opposed to the bread on your plate, you willingly relinquish everything to Him instead of continuing to grapple with it all by yourself.

Many believers are skimping with lean rations in their Christian life; little is harvested because little is sown. Little is shared because little is stored. Relief from the Lord is available, but it requires your participation. Commit each meal to the Lord; He will fill you so that your energy increases, your service expands, and your love overflows.

Praise God for the ways He has sustained you during your fast. This is more than skipping meals; it's about designating time to dine with the Lord. In this journey, you will gain much more than you lose.

With what are you currently struggling? Pour out your concerns; He will replenish you, replacing the bitter with the sweet.

Dinner

*"Come, all you who are thirsty, come to the waters;
and you who have no money, come, buy and eat! ..."*
(Isaiah 55:1)

✧ **Daily Bread** – Read: Psalm 36:8-9

The Lord's resources are limitless; however, we superficially spend a lot of time taking inventory of what we have and placing mental orders for what more we think we need. From our finite perspective, it seems we never have enough. We are always on the prowl for more, but God instructs us to be content in all things (Philippians 4:11-12, Hebrews 13:5). I believe that He Himself planted in us the desire for more and for better, and that He alone is the source of that great bounty. Our restricted human minds can not begin to fathom the wealth at our disposal if we commit our needs to the Lord.

During my 40-day fast, I realized that God did not want my sight to remain narrowed by earthly vision. He wanted my sight focused upwards. *"Set your minds on things above, not on earthly things."* (Colossians 3:2). The longer I fasted, the greater my eternal perspective became.

God admonishes His children not to stockpile unnecessary worldly goods. Instead, He points us towards the vast supply of joy and abundance that He has waiting for us in His heavenly storehouse. In the meantime, He is preparing you to accomplish His will in this alien land. Surrender your earthly desires, and ask the Lord to replace them with eternal ones.

DAY 16

Pain

Breakfast

"And the God of all grace, Who called you to His eternal glory in Christ, after you have suffered a little while, will Himself restore you and make you strong, firm and steadfast."
(1 Peter 5:10)

⚜ **Daily Bread** – Read: 1 Peter 4:12-13

Are you growing more aware of the pain and despair around you? Do you have newfound compassion for others even though you aren't experiencing the same illness or difficulty? During the course of my fast, as people confided in me about their individual sufferings, I really could empathize with much of their anguish because I was enduring similar distress and hardship. My body, my mind, and my spirit all developed a heightened consciousness of mercy.

Jesus, too, truly related to the suffering of those who reached out to Him because He Himself had been hungry, sick, weak, alone, and vulnerable. Fasting tends to do that; it opens your senses to all that is taking place around you. No longer blissfully – and ignorantly – unaware, once you receive God-given knowledge, you are divinely accountable to act on it.

My friend, who is in great pain, shared with me that she was sitting in her small group one day, listening to each person pray about coughs and sinus pain, and she could think of nothing except how silly their prayers sounded to her. As she sat there, tormented by chronic pain from a serious disorder, sniffling noses and watery eyes just seemed so trivial.

I completely understood what she was talking about. At the time, I was two weeks into my fast, and I knew my hunger pangs would not be satisfied any time soon, yet my kids were whining for lunch. It wasn't even 11:00 in the morning, and my husband had already put in his lunch order, too, requesting to eat promptly at noon. I was astonished! Were they all completely unaware that I had not eaten in days? How could they insist that I fill their bellies when mine was growling so loudly? "They just ate two hours ago!" I thought. "How can they possibly be hungry again?" Their self-absorption and thoughtlessness boggled my mind.

There are certainly degrees of adversity, and we must remember that the extent of one's suffering hinges on what God knows the individual can handle. A cough may appear to be a trifling inconvenience to some, but, to others, it may be a constant misery. We must be sensitive to all of the levels of suffering around us, and we must be careful not to trivialize anyone else's pain.

Pray that the Lord would make you more perceptive to the needs of those around you, and diligently pray for them no matter how simple their requests may seem. Pray that those who are suffering from chronic diseases and perpetual pain may receive an extra dose of God's grace and mercy.

Lunch

"Blessed is the man who perseveres under trial, because when he has stood the test, he will receive the crown of life that God has promised to those who love Him."
(James 1:12)

⚜ **Daily Bread** – Read: James 1:2-5

I recently watched an episode of *Little House on the Prairie* with my daughters. I so enjoyed that television program when I was young, and I'm grateful for the reruns. In this particular episode, Dr. Baker explained to Charles Ingalls that pain is God's way of alerting us that something is wrong. His statement is so true! We often see pain as a nuisance – a road block preventing us from getting where we want to go. But, from God's perspective, the trials of life do not derail us but, instead, get us back on track. Through our hardships, He builds in us a stronger faith, so we can withstand more difficult trials ahead. He teaches us to trust in Him; we learn that nothing is really in our control but that nothing is ever out of His. We develop perseverance and patience; our hearts swell with fresh mercy.

Most television shows today actually desensitize viewers. Blatant violence, profanity, and sexuality are prevalent in many programs, dulling our senses until we longer find them offensive. Though we can easily turn a deaf ear and a blind eye to what is broadcast in our living rooms or in the local movie theater, tuning out our own afflictions proves to be more difficult. Only when we personally experience difficulty, trials, and traumas, can we truly relate to the suffering of others.

The enemy connives to isolate you in your suffering. Do you feel forsaken in your current struggle? Share it with someone, and ask for intercessory prayer. Proverbs 27:17 reassures, *"As iron sharpens iron, so one man sharpens another."* Ask the Lord to provide a friend in whom you can confide. Pray for discernment to recognize others whom you can encourage.

Dinner

" 'I have told you these things, so that in Me you may have peace. In this world you will have trouble. But take heart! I have overcome the world.' "
(John 16:33)

⚜ **Daily Bread** – Read: Romans 8:18

No matter how much difficulty you encounter in this world, you can rest assured that you will never experience the depth of pain that Jesus endured. He came in human flesh to prove that He is a God who understands human sufferings. He knows exactly what you are going through. He gave up a heavenly throne, and chose to live in this world to suffer as we never could – so we never would.

Compare the level of your pain to the cross – you will never suffer as Jesus did. Compare the longevity of your pain to eternity – you will not suffer for long. In the meantime, whatever your pain, suffer it for the glory of God.

Pray that as you endure your present sufferings, your choices glorify God. When you speak of your difficulties to others, share how the Lord is working in your life and how He is caring for and comforting you. Lift up those around you who are also enduring earthly trials and tribulations.

DAY 17

Listen

Breakfast

"Whether you turn to the right or to the left, your ears will hear a Voice behind you, saying, 'This is the way; walk in it.' "
(Isaiah 30:21)

⚜ **Daily Bread** – Read: 1 Corinthians 2:13-16

"My stomach is really howling this morning, and it's easy to get distracted by that annoying noise. But, I am enjoying reading a devotional that a friend gave me on writing. It is entitled For the Write Reason by Marybeth Whalen. It has really encouraged me to press on with the dream that God gave me to write and to continue journaling throughout this fast. It has been good confirmation for the path God has put before me, and I'm just pressing in to learn what God wants to show me. I don't want to get ahead of His plans. I know He is really working on peeling off my other layers, helping me become more honest and open. Today, I am sending a poem I wrote to a friend who needs prayer and encouragement." (My Fasting Journal, Day 17).

God finds many ways to reach out and speak to you. Fasting disciplines you to better communicate with the Lord as you read the Scriptures and listen for His revelations. The deeper you dig, the more you unearth. He speaks volumes through His Word, and, if you diligently study it, He will open your eyes and ears to new insights and fresh knowledge every single day.

Be aware, too, of other ways He speaks to you – through an unexpected phone call or e-mail from a friend, or through a confirming book, devotional, or card. Even a song that gives voice to a Scripture the Lord has laid on your heart is a sweet gift. He is always speaking; you must learn to discern His voice.

Your sacrifice and desire to follow the Lord delights Him. What confirmations has He given you this past week to indicate His pleasure?

_____
_____
_____
_____
_____

Lunch

"My sheep listen to My voice; I know them, and they follow Me." – John 10:27

⚜ **Daily Bread** – Read: Matthew 6:6-13

Our conversations with God can easily turn one-sided, and I fear our Heavenly Father often receives a glut of verbal downloads. We request, we demand, we thank, we praise, and then we hurry on to our busy task of living. What if we just closed our eyes, set aside the day's distractions, gave our own voices a rest, and just listened to the Lord? What would He sound like? Would we even recognize Him if we heard Him speak?

The Lord gives us a perfect example of prayer in Matthew 6. It's sandwiched right in between giving and fasting. God instructs us to do all three – giving to the needy, praying, and fasting – in secret. That doesn't necessarily mean that we shouldn't tell anyone – the enemy would love for us to keep our obedience to ourselves, and isolation is one of his favorite tactics to discourage us and immobilize us. It does mean to keep your motives pure and remain humble. We do these things for the glory of God, not for the praise of men.

This afternoon, find a quiet retreat where you can enjoy God's creation. Pray the Lord's Prayer, and then close your eyes, open your ears, and listen. What is He saying to you today?

_____
_____
_____
_____
_____
_____
_____
_____
_____
_____
_____
_____

Dinner

"Here I am! I stand at the door and knock. If anyone hears My voice and opens the door,
I will come in and eat with him and he with Me."
(Revelation 3:20)

⚜ **Daily Bread** – Read: Luke 10:38-42

Have you ever received a phone call when you were sitting down to eat? Have you intended a quick trip into the grocery store only to meet someone who wants to engage in a long conversation? Have your children tugged at you, begging you to come see their newest work of art (and their big mess that you will have to clean up later) when you were trying to get dinner on the table?

So many incidents like these are dismissed as frustrating distractions, but, what if you looked beyond your initial annoyance and saw something more? That phone call is, in fact, a friend in need who could really use an encouraging word from a godly source. That person in the grocery store is a former church member who hasn't participated or attended in ten years because of a misunderstanding. That child with the messy artwork is just trying to share with you, hoping for some undivided attention and unconditional love.

We spend a lot of time shopping for food, preparing food, and eating food. So much of our time revolves around meals, and many of our distractions come at those same times. Try to see the interruptions from a different perspective, and embrace them as Divine appointments set by the Father. They may seem inconvenient, but they're actually right on time according to His schedule.

Be willing to interrupt your routine, and seize your God-given opportunities to represent His love each day. Pray for the grace to put the Lord's schedule before your own.

DAY 18

Learning to Fly

Breakfast

"But our citizenship is in heaven. And we eagerly await a Savior from there, the Lord Jesus Christ, Who, by the power that enables Him to bring everything under His control, will transform our lowly bodies so that they will be like His glorious body."
(Philippians 3:20-21)

⚜ Daily Bread – Read: 2 Corinthians 5:17-21

One morning, my two daughters asked me to come outside and look at a big bug attached to our split rail fence in the backyard. As we got closer, I realized that the bug was, in fact, a cocoon. I told the girls that eventually, a beautiful butterfly would emerge from its plain, gray, shapeless covering. They were very excited at the prospect of seeing a butterfly's birth but were disappointed that I couldn't tell them the exact day or time it would happen.

I've enjoyed serving in children's ministry for many years and have used the story of the butterfly on a number of occasions, especially around Easter, as an object lesson illustrating Christ's death, burial and resurrection.

We constantly die to ourselves in order to reveal Lord Jesus in us. We cast aside our old sin natures in order to birth holy and righteous ones. Just as ugly caterpillars transform into glorious creatures, we surrender our unseemly, sin-stained selves, metamorphosing into beautiful, resplendent images of God.

We seem very small, plain, and insignificant in this big world, but God sees our potential greatness, beauty, and relevance. For now, we inch along in the dirt, but He plans for us to soar with the eagles. Allow Him to do the necessary work in order to transform your earth-bound self into a heaven-bound one. Be patient with Him as He is patient with you. Thank Him for His transforming handiwork in your life.

_____
_____
_____
_____
_____

Lunch

"What wings are to a bird, and sails are to a ship, so is prayer to the soul."
– Corrie ten Boom

⚜ **Daily Bread** – Read: Isaiah 40:31

One day, my four-year-old daughter put on her beautiful blue and lavender dress-up butterfly wings and began jumping up and down on my bed. The walls in my bedroom are painted sky blue, and bed is covered with cloud white linens. She looked like a beautiful angel bouncing all over heaven. She proceeded to ask a question in between each jump: "Mommy… how… do…we…fly?"

Her question was so innocent, and I didn't want to burst her bubble by telling her that we can't fly. So, I answered with, "You've just got to keep jumping." That made her happy until she decided to test out her new skills and jumped right off the bed into the air. Her hard landing didn't discourage her; she exclaimed that she must need more practice. I had to laugh.

When our children fail or fall, we encourage them to get back up and try again. When they tumble to ground while attempting to ride a bicycle without training wheels for the first time, we cheer them on and applaud their willingness to hop right back on despite scraped knees and bloodied elbows. Our excitement thrills them, and they delight in pleasing us.

I think God must feel the same way about us as we feel about our children. He watches over us, cheering us on, cringing when we fall, and smiling broadly when we pick ourselves up and take another risk. He looks on tenderly as we dirty ourselves during our feeble attempts and beams when we dust ourselves off and carry on. Like a proud father who sees his child finally succeed in riding his bike all the way to the end of the driveway, our heavenly Father stands amazed, His heart brimming with love for His precious, prized child.

It's odd to think that we could amaze God, but we do please Him when we persevere through unfamiliar and uncomfortable assignments, trusting Him for the end result, and believing that we can do everything through Him who gives us strength (Philippians 4:13). Our humble faithfulness is His great delight.

Did you give God a reason to smile on you today? Thank Him for His watchful eye and His gentle hand. In difficult circumstances, pray for His strength to try, try, and try again, and make yourself available to cheer on the efforts of another.

Dinner

"Take the helmet of salvation and the sword of the Spirit, which is the word of God. And pray in the Spirit on all occasions with all kinds of prayers and requests. With this in mind, be alert and always keep on praying for all the saints."
(Ephesians 6:17-18)

⚜ **Daily Bread** – Read: Exodus 19:4-5

Sometimes, our own fears keep us from staying the course and accomplishing our God-given missions. Other times, the discouraging voices of those around us paralyze us and prevent us from moving forward. Often, the people behind the voices are the ones who generate our worry.

The enemy uses negative people to condemn and discourage us. One negative voice in the company of a hundred positive ones can rip right through our best intentions, deflating them in an instant. Why does this one destructive force carry so much power? Consider that the enemy wages his greatest war in our minds. If he can get a foothold into your thoughts, he has gained significant ground. It is the enemy's desire that we remain grounded, with wings clipped, so we gain no other view than our present human perspective.

God desires that in all things we see Him. It is critical to protect your mind from enemy infiltration. The Lord called the Israelites to remember all that He had done for them and He desires the same from us today. He knows when we fill our minds with His thoughts, and reflect on all the promises He has faithfully fulfilled, we will have no reason to do anything else but hope in Him. Fill your mind with Christ; memorize Scripture, and build up your artillery with His Word. It's the greatest weapon to retreat the enemy.

God has great plans for you; the enemy wants to thwart them, like the bully he is, by trying to keep you on the ground. Jesus calls you to stand firm, remembering that *"the One who is in you is greater than the one who is in the world"* (1 John 4:4), and soar on eagle's wings.

Do not allow the enemy to gain any ground; protect his biggest target – your mind. Think only godly thoughts as Paul encourages in Philippians 4:8: *"… whatever is true, whatever is noble, whatever is right, whatever is pure, whatever is lovely, whatever is admirable – if anything is excellent or praiseworthy – think about such things."* Fill your mind with the Word of God, for the enemy can not stand where Christ reigns (Luke 10:18-20).

Ask God to help you guard your thoughts. Memorize His Word, and focus your eyes on Him. Stand firm in the battles, remembering that Jesus wins the war.

_____
_____
_____
_____
_____
_____
_____
_____

DAY 19
Persistent Prayer

Breakfast

"The prayer of a righteous man is powerful and effective."
(James 5:16b)

⚜ **Daily Bread** – Read: James 5:13-16

"We had a praise report today in our Bible study. The woman who had been critical and discouraging to one of our sisters in Christ had an amazing change of heart. We have all been praying that our sister would stand firm, remain faithful, and stay encouraged. And, we have been praying for a softening of heart and an openness to God's love for the woman with the critical spirit. Thank you, Lord, for these victories that we have in You." (My Fasting Journal, Day 20).

God is so good when we pray and submit our requests before Him. He is faithful to respond, and although His answers don't always come as quickly as this particular one did, they always arrive in His perfect timing. He requires us to remain faithful, leaving the details to Him.

In *Experiencing the Heart of Jesus*, Max Lucado observed, "The power of prayer does not depend on the one who makes the prayer but on the One who hears the prayer."

Our power lies in the submission of our prayer. Attempting to figure out a solution under our own power is futile work. We have no power, but we do have the privilege of being the child of a loving Father who hears our prayers and answers them according to His perfect will.

The burdens, trials, and difficulties that we face are but a small part of His great Kingdom plan. We can not begin to comprehend the heavenly work now in progress which will shape the landscape of the future. Our prayers hold great importance; what and whom we pray for today has the potential to change lives tomorrow.

Who knows what seeds our prayers planted in the critical spirit of this woman? Only God sees the condition of her heart and knows exactly what she needs. Our sister remained firm in Christ despite the enemy's attempts to send her scurrying in the opposite direction, and it was a significant victory. The venomous words may have come from the mouth of the woman, but they were planted by the enemy.

We are warriors in God's great army, and we must remain faithful, stand firm, and pray without ceasing for everyone whom the Lord brings into our lives – the good, the bad, and the ugly. God only knows the lives that will be transformed because of our faithful prayers.

_____
_____
_____
_____
_____
_____
_____
_____
_____
_____

Lunch

"Pray continually."
(1 Thessalonians 5:17)

⚜ **Daily Bread** – Read: 1 John 5:14-15

We must persist in our prayers even though we don't receive His answers right away. His timing is one reason I enjoy keeping a prayer journal, and one reason why you're recording your thoughts and prayers in this journal. I have revisited my own 40-day fasting and prayer journal and recorded the answers to every single prayer I had written. Some are amazing answers to seemingly impossible prayers, and some responses are just the beginning of what I recognize as God's work.

By writing our prayers to God, we have an encouraging record not only of His faithfulness but also of our personal journey with Him. I enjoy rereading my prayer journals, remembering old concerns, people for whom I prayed, lives that were changed, and places that God took me.

Looking back on His faithfulness helps me look forward to His promises. I know that regardless of the challenges in this life, I have a Divine blueprint of His work in my life, and it serves as a constant encouragement in my current Christian walk. Because of the past, I will persevere in the present and forge ahead to the future.

The Bible is the paramount written record of God's faithfulness. From Genesis to Revelation, the pages contain the stories of real people: their trials and their triumphs, their difficulties and their deliverance, and, throughout it all, their prayers and God's promises.

I love to read the 11th chapter of Hebrews, which is often referred to as the Hall of Fame of the Faithful. This chapter remembers some of God's faithful, obedient children who walked with Him and lived for Him. None of them received God's promise on earth, but all of them lived in hope and faith. They received their reward and one day will see the completion of His promise. The best is yet to be.

"Let us not become weary in doing good, for at the proper time we will reap a harvest if we do not give up." (Galatians 6:9). For whom are you praying without ceasing? God is faithful and will answer your prayers with Divine precision.

_____
_____

Dinner

*"And the people all tried to touch Him,
because power was coming from Him and healing them all."*
(Luke 6:19)

⚜ **Daily Bread** – Read: Mark 5:25-34

If Jesus felt the power go out of Him when the sick woman just barely touched the hem of His cloak, I wonder how He feels when we submit our prayers to Him? Do our fervent prayers grab His attention in such a way that He can't help but turn an ear to those who are crying out to Him? Does He physically feel the drain when we humbly and earnestly reach out for His power?

Job's friends ridiculed him; they told him he suffered because he had little faith. But, it's not the size of our faith that heals us; it's the size of our God. Jesus said we only need faith the size of a mustard seed to move mountains (Matthew 17:20). If God gives us no more than we can handle, it stands to reason that those with great faith can endure greater suffering.

Ultimately, God is God; we are not. We don't hold the power; He does. By clinging to Him, and by humbly submitting our prayers for His Divine consideration, we can rest in our dependence on Him, trusting in His power, mercy, and grace.

Where do you feel His power in your life?

DAY 20

Verbal Vomit

Breakfast

"A gentle answer turns away wrath, but a harsh word stirs up anger."
(Proverbs 15:1)

♣ **Daily Bread** – Read: Romans 8:5-8

"Okay, so I lost it this morning. It was destined to happen at some point. There was a great build-up, like a volcano ready to erupt. I thought I was managing this time of fasting quite well, but I think that's where I messed up – the word "I". This is not about me, but, somehow, I keep coming back to me. And, when I get my eyes off of the One Who is really in control, I lose control. What a mess! Something as simple as my husband getting on me for not being ready on time to take the kids to their sporting events became the straw that broke the camel's back. I was having bathroom problems. My tardiness was the result of something out of my control. This fasting is not without its physical downsides, and I'm not talking about weight loss – that is hardly a bad thing. I'm talking about volcanic eruptions, and I don't mean the one that just spewed all over my husband and children. Regardless, it was a mess – coming out both ends of me, and I think more garbage came out of my mouth than out of the other end. It was not a pretty sight. The good news is that the garbage is out. The bad news is that I had some cleaning up to do. Lord, help me not lose control like that again. Please keep my attitude in check even when everyone else's isn't. I need Your strength." (My Fasting Journal, Day 21).

It's true! Your body will go through some detoxification, and your spirit will, too. Pray that the Lord will guide you and help you prudently release the garbage in your life: anger, pride, control, weakness – whatever it may be. Commit your mess to your Lord. Trust Him to bring it to the surface and eliminate it from your life for good.

_____
_____
_____
_____
_____
_____
_____
_____

Lunch

"You intended to harm me, but God intended it for good to accomplish what is now being done, the saving of many lives."
(Genesis 50:20)

⚜ **Daily Bread** – Read: Luke 6:45

I thought I had issues. I ran into a friend who just downloaded all over me. I wasn't aware that I had a sign on my forehead that read "Local Refuse Site", but, apparently, I was the lucky recipient of a savage spewing of what I like to call "verbal vomit".

Do you have friends like that? I use the word "friend" lightly; with friends like that, who needs enemies, right? But, I think you know the type: they are sick of everyone and everything. They are right; the world is wrong. Everyone else is to blame. Instead of laying it at Jesus' feet, they lay it all on you.

What is interesting to me about verbal vomit is how quickly and violently it erupts. It's as if the venom has been building up for so long, it can not be contained a second more, and, all of a sudden – there she blows! The difficult thing about being the recipient of such an explosion is trying to remain composed and Christ-like under the verbal assault.

I've been there several times before (lucky me!), and I found myself debating whether I should laugh or cry. Either one might have caused an unintended and unwanted reaction by the spewer. If I laughed, she might be offended. If I cried, she might be emboldened to spew some more.

So, in this instance, I did what any mature believer would do. I silently screamed in my head, "WHAT WAS THAT ALL ABOUT?!" And, then, I began to pray. After being on the receiving end of such an attack, it's easy for the spewee to take the outburst personally – to feel completely violated, dumped on, and taken advantage of. But, I took a few steps back and considered my own eruption earlier in the day. I remembered that the source of my toxic discharge was built entirely upon something other than my poor husband and children, although they took the hit from the blast. I decided that I needed to give my friend the benefit of the doubt.

I silently thanked the Lord that He was entrusting this explosion to me (since I had my own personal experience in the matter), and I prayed for my friend, asking God to give me the right words of encouragement for her. I'm sure our conversation would have ended quite differently had I not responded to her in Christ. Thankfully, I recognized the enemy's handiwork, and I wasn't about to give him the victory. God got the glory, as He should have.

Whether you've been the dumper or the dumpee, ask God to show you how to prayerfully keep your actions and attitudes in check whenever you face such acid attacks.

_____
_____
_____
_____
_____
_____
_____

Dinner

"Blessed is the man who perseveres under trial, because when he has stood the test, he will receive the crown of life that God has promised to those who love Him."
(James 1:12)

⚜ **Daily Bread** – Read: Ephesians 6:10-18

While I'm not thrilled to be the recipient of verbal vomit, I am grateful that I've grown in my ability to respond in a manner that pleases my Heavenly Father. When His children thoughtfully and prayerfully ask to see circumstances from His perspective, He is delighted. Jesus provided the way for us during His earthly ministry; He Himself was dumped upon and spit upon – and that was just the beginning of His suffering.

James 1:2-5 encourages, *"Consider it pure joy, my brothers, whenever you face trials of many kinds, because you know that the testing of your faith develops perseverance. Perseverance must finish its work so that you may be mature and complete, not lacking anything. If any of you lacks wisdom, he should ask God, Who gives generously to all without finding fault, and it will be given to him."*

Notice that James writes "when", not "if". When I'm under attack, I think of Jesus, but sometimes that's easier said than done. I sustained another raging retch from a friend at church one Sunday. When she finished downloading on me, I tried my best to appear unaffected by her assault; I knew that she did not intend it for me, so I struggled to see her through God's eyes, as a precious child who was having a really bad day. I had no idea what triggered by friend's episode, but, whatever it was, I was in the right place at the right time (wrong place at the wrong time?!) to absorb the torrent. Functioning on the residual fumes from a sleepless night myself, I was barely equipped to handle her outburst, but I did my best to encourage her, and, then, I ran for the bathroom to cry and talk with the Lord.

When I emerged, red-nosed, blotchy-faced, and puffy-eyed, one of the volunteers noticed how bad I looked. (Gee, thanks!) She suggested that I call it a day and go home. That's when it hit me; the enemy was on the prowl, discouraging me and scheming to incapacitate me. I knew instantly that I would not surrender to him that day, so I defiantly marched up the hallway to shepherd a group of first graders.

What happened next made the entire ordeal worthwhile. When the church service ended, as I was walking to my car, I heard a little voice calling out to me, "Ms. Traci! Ms. Traci!" I turned to find one of those first graders running after me with his arms open wide. I stopped to let him catch up with me, and he ran straight into me, offering a huge hug and a big smile. Then, he said simply, "Ms. Traci, I love you." I cried all the way home that day, partly in response to the earlier attack, but mostly in relief for the end reward. In the arms of that little boy, I felt the love of God embracing me, telling me, " *'Well done, good and faithful servant!'* " (Matthew 25:21).

In His infinite wisdom, God knows exactly what we can handle and exactly what we need. From raging words to redeeming ones, the Lord is with us through it all. I suppose I should be glad that the enemy considers my Christian witness a big enough threat to warrant his time and trouble. Praise God that the power that I have in Christ leaves the enemy impotent.

Thank God for all the ways He helps you stand in the face of your enemy, and praise Him for all the ways He confirms that His presence.

DAY 21

Words

Breakfast

"Do not merely listen to the word, and so deceive yourselves. Do what it says."
(James 1:22)

⚜ **Daily Bread** – Read: John 1:1-5

At God's word, light appeared (Genesis 1), a stormy sea calmed (Matthew 8), and Lazarus rose from the dead (John 11). Words have tremendous power; therefore, we should take great care to utilize them in a manner befitting Christ Jesus.

It is significant that Jesus Himself was called "the Word": *"The Word became flesh and made His dwelling among us."* – John 1:14

The name of Jesus is, by far, the greatest word ever uttered. For thousands of years, He was a Word of Promise; He then was the Promise fulfilled. At the time of His birth, there had been 400 years of silence without a word from God. One would think that the entire world would have been straining to hear a fresh word from Him, but, for those 400 years, the people then did just what many of us are doing today. They lived life and ignored God. Instead of being watchful, they were just being wasteful, and, when Jesus entered the world in the form of a tiny baby, the world missed it.

Today, consider the parts of your life that keep you the busiest. Are they God-centered or self-centered? The Lord dwells among us wherever we are: at school, on the job, in the neighborhood, and everywhere in between. Do not relegate Him only to Sunday morning worship or weekday gatherings with other believers.

What areas of your life need to include Christ? Do not be silent about your faith. If you don't speak the name of Jesus, who will? Pray that you share everything in your life with Jesus, and pray that you share His Word with everyone in your life.

_____
_____
_____
_____
_____
_____
_____
_____

Lunch

"How sweet are Your words to my taste, sweeter than honey to my mouth!"
(Psalm 119:103)

⚜ **Daily Bread** – Read: Ephesians 5:1-2

The Word of God is His offering to us. What a gracious gift! It is a gift that keeps on giving; the Lord desires His children to emulate the life of Christ, and our directions are carefully detailed in the Bible.

Jesus ministered in amazing calmness and serenity. Although throngs of people followed Him wherever He went, He never pushed them away, ignored them, or told them to go away and leave Him alone. He knew His time on earth was short, and He had to make every minute count. He accomplished His Father's will by living to die, and He lived each moment in full awareness of His mission, making the most of every opportunity because eternal life for His followers hinged on His obedience.

The life He lived, the death He died, and the resurrection He purposed all compose the very foundation of our faith. He remained faithful, not only in the ultimate fulfillment of His great sacrifice but also in the daily following of His Heavenly Father. He needed to leave us not only a hope for the future but also a model for the present. He is not to be admired; He is to be emulated.

Jesus always spoke Truth and always related to others at their level. He always put others before Himself but never prioritized anyone above His Heavenly Father. In the Garden of Gethsemane, Jesus prayed so earnestly that *"His sweat was like drops of blood"* (Luke 22:44). I believe that His anguish extended beyond the thought of His impending brutal death and included the despairing knowledge that He had to leave us behind.

His love was so great for us that He chose to die for us, but I think He mourned the thought of leaving us alone in this dark world. He experienced first-hand the difficulties His children faced – and continue to face – from living *"as aliens and strangers in the world"* (1 Peter 2:11).

Jesus prayed for His followers then just as He prays for us today (John 17:20-26), desiring that we keep an eternal perspective when we have troublesome choices to make. And, remembering how many people still need to experience His love, He calls us to serve as His hands and feet for as long as our life continues on this earth.

Today, pray for those who need Jesus, and pray that you may always represent the love and light of Jesus Christ to everyone around you.

Dinner

"The tongue has the power of life and death…"
(Proverbs 18:21)

⚜ **Daily Bread** – Read: Ephesians 4:29-32

During my fast, my women's small group was studying *The Patriarchs*[1] by Beth Moore. I have studied Genesis several times, and I truly enjoyed this particular glimpse of the early faithful (but definitely not perfect!) leaders of the faith.

It was an Old Testament tradition for a father to bless his children, and the most important one was designated for his first-born son. Blessings were powerful and carefully worded, and they extended throughout generations. Isaac's son, Jacob, betrayed his father in order to receive his older brother's blessing. Esau and Jacob were twins, but Esau entered the world before his brother, technically earning the first-born birthright. With assistance from his mother, Rebekah, Jacob stole the birthright right out from under his brother, who wasn't really paying very close attention at the time. Prophesied in Genesis 25:23, Jacob's deception changed the course of history.

The Power of Spoken Blessings by Bill Gothard stresses the importance of vocalizing our blessings. The tradition of blessing has been largely ignored and underutilized by the church as has the tradition of fasting. I've found, though, that when my children are not acting appropriately, replacing (or at least supplementing) my words of correction to them with words of blessing over them dramatically improves their attitudes and behaviors. They respond more readily to loving affirmation than to harsh criticism.

When we pray specific Scriptures over our children and loved ones, they absorb Truth into their very being. By speaking encouraging and sanctifying words, we lift the spirits of those whom we cherish. Their confidence surges, their esteem swells, and their desire to behave in a Christ-like manner strengthens.

In Christ, our words can transform lives. When we say His name and speak His Word, we have the power to illuminate the darkness with His Light. Saturate your heart and mind with His Word, and pray that the overflow will spill onto those around you. Tonight, write a blessing for the loved ones in your life.

Broken and Weak

"The LORD is close to the brokenhearted and saves those who are crushed in spirit."
(Psalm 34:18)

Christian artist Natalie Grant wrote a beautiful song entitled "The Real Me" in which she sings the refrain: "But you see the real me/Hiding in my skin, broken from within/Unveil me completely/I'm loosening my grasp/There's no need to mask my frailty/Cause you see the real me."

This song symbolized the fourth week of my fast. I'd established a good routine of prayer and study, my bodily functions had stabilized, the Lord had stripped my many layers, and He was ready to take me to an unexpected place. In Jeremiah 33:3, the Lord promises, " 'Call to Me and I will answer you and tell you great and unsearchable things you do not know.' "

If you truly seek Him, desiring to learn more, buckle your seat belt because He will lead you on some pretty exciting and surprising adventures. Some will be wonderful and inspiring; others may seem painful for the moment, but eventually and triumphantly reveal His glory. The latter was true for me as I finally surrendered a part of myself to the Lord that I had tried to hide for many years.

I'd spent the better part of my life trying to be the best person that I could be, giving 110% to everything I did, being as professional, courteous, patient, and kind as humanly possible. (As I type this, I see two dead giveaways in that sentence: "I" and "humanly possible".) I perfected an air of strength and labeled it the power of God.

However, the more I strove for perfectionism, the more of a façade it became. I did a great job of acting like someone who had all her proverbial ducks in a row, but, in actuality, what looked good on the outside wasn't what was going on in the inside.

God was in control, and He was always leading me, but I wasn't always completely honest with myself – or others – about how much help I really needed. I didn't want to burden anyone unnecessarily, and, I reasoned that if I took care of everything myself, I wouldn't have to clean up the mess of unfinished business from careless people to whom I had delegated responsibilities. I truly did not trust people. I'd had way too many people drop the ball, miss the boat, and just plain disappoint me over the years. It was easier to adopt the philosophy, "If you want something done right, you've got to do it yourself."

The problem, though, when one tries to carry all the balls oneself, is that the burden eventually becomes too big to bear, and then, the one pretending to be perfect is the one dropping the balls. I've come to realize that the less you appear to need people, the less they even bother to show up and offer assistance. And, the more strength I appeared to exude, the more intimidating I seemed. Why would anyone want to help if their service wasn't required or welcomed? I set the bar so high, people didn't even try to measure up.

If we're working in our own strength instead of Christ's, we present a very skewed picture of Him and what he requires of his followers. The truth is that He does His greatest work through our weakness. In 2 Corinthians 11:30, Paul expresses, "If I must boast, I will boast of the things that show my weakness." He understood that through our weaknesses, God's glory is magnified.

Our ability is not as important as our availability. God uses those whose hearts are willing. Think of some of the unexpected heroes in the Bible; King David was just young shepherd boy when God chose him. God isn't looking for people who fit some worldly expectation of what a leading man or leading lady should be. *"…The LORD does not look at the things man looks at. Man looks at the outward appearance, but the LORD looks at the heart."* (1 Samuel 16:7).

God wants to strip our thin, poorly applied veneers and reveal His true beauty and strength. His best makeovers begin with those whom the world scorns. His most significant work is accomplished through our broken pieces. We should not care what others think; we should do what pleases Him. The Lord will create a masterpiece if we surrender our cheap imitation.

DAY 22

Naked

Breakfast

"Therefore, if anyone is in Christ, he is a new creation; the old has gone, the new has come!"
(2 Corinthians 5:17)

✣ **Daily Bread** – Read: 2 Corinthians 4:16-18

I've read that the most dangerous place to be is in the center of God's will. The moment someone accepts Christ, the storms roll in. The enemy wages a full force attack, and God, in His infinite wisdom, allows us to weather the storm so that we will recognize our own weakness and cling to Him. Each battering wind peels away another sheet of our unnecessary and unattractive layers until we are completely raw and exposed. It is then that God unleashes His power in our lives, and His Spirit, no longer hidden beneath our cloaks of sin, can finally and freely shine through.

The Lord knows that to stand against the opposition in this world, we must be adequately prepared and well dressed. In clothing us for battle, He works from the inside out. When we are suited up in the full armor of God and dressed in His righteousness, we are properly attired to withstand the gathering storms.

We are in enemy territory, and we will gain more ground outfitted in God's character and strength. Protected within the folds of the Creator of the world, we have no reason to fear the advances of the enemy. *"…clothe yourself with strength. Put on your garments of splendor…"* (Isaiah 52:1).

Do not brace the storms in your life thinly dressed. *"Rather, clothe yourselves with the Lord Jesus Christ…"* (Romans 13:14). Let the Lord cover you – not so you can cower under Him but so you can stand firm and triumphant in His royal wrapping. Ask Him to strip away your shame and layer you with His love and strength.

_____
_____
_____
_____

Lunch

"He reveals deep and hidden things; He knows what lies in darkness, and light dwells with Him."
(Daniel 2:22)

♣ **Daily Bread** — Read: Matthew 23:25-28

In this world, appearance is everything. Acceptance equals the hippest clothes, the coolest car, and the edgiest haircut. Those who have "it" are in the club; those who don't are not. She who has the least wrinkles, the smallest waistline, and the best tan wins. We perfect the outside but neglect the inside. Our superficial masks disguise our crumbling foundations, but the Lord sees our inner decay.

Sometimes the more dressed-up and put-together we appear, the more we're trying to hide. Instead of hastily tucking our problems inside our polished appearance and pretending they don't exist, the Lord desires that we pull them out, try them on for size, and see for ourselves how ill-fitting they really are. Our denial is disfiguring, but our false front is disguising the true fatal flaw: our powerlessness.

Without God, we can do nothing. You can dress us up, but you can't take us out! Our empty and artificial shells are useless to Him, but, if we allow Him to redress us in His majesty and strength, we take on a new form, courageously clothed in Christ.

When we live a lie, we break God's law. Our lives should reflect His transparent Truth, but we hide so much beneath our surfaces, that His Light can not shine through our opaqueness. God wants to peel off our masks and go right to the root of our weaknesses. There's no sense in superficially dressing our wounds when the Spirit of the Great Healer is living inside of us! We must stop disguising, denying, and defending our feeble attempts to be what we are not. In John 7:24, Jesus cautioned, *"Stop judging by mere appearances and make a right judgment."*

What masks do you wear? We all have something to hide. We live in a fallen world trying to cover its imperfection with a flimsy façade built on nothing solid, but *"…God does not judge by external appearance…"* (Galatians 2:6). Ask God for the courage to uncover your weaknesses and reveal the real you. He accepts you just as you are. Try to see yourself through His loving eyes.

Dinner

"…Who told you that you were naked?…"
(Genesis 3:11)

♣ **Daily Bread** – Read: Job 1:21

From the moment we are born, we cover our naked flesh. We've been conditioned that our nakedness is inappropriate and indecent, and we blush at exposing ourselves. In the first book of the Bible, Adam and Eve sinned and realized they were naked; God created a sin-covering for them, and we've been working diligently to improve our cover-up ever since.

No matter how fancy the fabric, how fine the tailoring, and how fashionable the accessories, sin is still sin, and we can't cover it up. The only canopy that can truly cover our sin is the same one that exposes it: the Truth of Jesus. The Truth of His love and sacrifice blankets us, and His precious blood washes us whiter than snow and wool (Isaiah 1:18).

One day, when we join Christ in paradise, we will receive a glorious robe of righteousness (Isaiah 61:10) that He custom-made, just our size. In the meantime, we must not live on this earth camouflaged in sin and shame. Be released from the cloak of darkness by accepting the atoning sacrifice of Jesus' death and resurrection. Your sin has already been paid in full; why are you still paying the bill?

Express your gratitude to the Lord for saving you, cleansing you, and replacing your sin habit with His garment of salvation. *"Have nothing to do with the fruitless deeds of darkness, but rather expose them."* (Ephesians 5:11). Pray that those who are still exposed to sin through their threadbare costume will accept the generous covering provided upon their acceptance of Jesus' glorious gift of salvation.

DAY 23

Labor Pains

Breakfast

"...I am again in the pains of childbirth until Christ is formed in you..."
(Galatians 4:19)

✣ **Daily Bread** – Read: Colossians 1:29

"God is trying to bring something out that is deep in the core of our being; He wants us to face and release it so He can give birth to something new and amazing and beautiful in our lives – a healing, a testimony, a ministry. But, often, we don't want to go the distance or work through the pain to get to the place that God wants to take us. The journey just seems too long, or we do not have the strength to continue. But, much like childbirth, God tries to show us the beauty that is on the other side of our present turmoil. It is a question of faith: are we willing to believe His promises and let Him carry us through to the other side, or are we going to trust the limited view of what we see and throw in the towel?" (My Fasting Journal, Day 23).

Life is full of difficulty. Anyone who says that life in Christ is devoid of challenges should research the accounts of the early disciples and remember the persecution they suffered while sharing the gospel message. Oppression occurs today, as well, in the lives of those who follow Jesus.

When you accepted Christ as your Savior, His Spirit came to dwell within you, and the Lord's Holy transformation began. Unlike pregnancy, this metamorphosis lasts longer than nine months; it continues to develop for a lifetime. But, much like labor pains, the Lord will indicate when you are to give birth to the work He is creating in you.

As you consider the struggles before you, they may seem unbearable, but think of them as part of a birthing process. The extreme pain will push you along, but it will eventually end, resulting in the most beautiful creation you've ever witnessed. *"...Always give yourselves fully to the work of the Lord, because you know that your labor in the Lord is not in vain."* (1 Corinthians 15:58). Pray for endurance, and ask the Lord for focus. He will coach you!

Lunch

"…it is God who works in you to will and to act according to His good purpose."
(Philippians 2:12)

⚜ **Daily Bread** – Read: Philippians 4:13

When I was in labor with my children, I claimed Philippians 4:13 to help me endure the birthing process. I had been coached to select a focal point on which I could concentrate during the course of my labor. I chose to fixate on Jesus, and He definitely made His presence known. My dedicated focus tapped into His strength, provided to me through the indwelling of His Holy Spirit. With His help, I knew I could endure anything, and I specifically asked for no anesthetics or other medicines because I wanted Him to be my prescription and my salve.

The birth of my second child was quick; I was already in intense labor when we left the house, and we were urgently rushing to the hospital. It was the middle of the night, and, on our way to the hospital, we had to stop at a friend's house to drop off my firstborn. In the meantime, my labor was swiftly progressing. As my husband sped down the highway, I was very thankful that the hour was late, and few cars were on the road. I knew the baby was about to arrive, and I felt Jesus clearing our way and protecting us from an accident – or a speeding ticket! I began praying my labor verse out loud and must have repeated it over 100 times before we finally made it to the hospital. We arrived at the hospital just moments before our beautiful baby girl arrived. It was by far the quickest and easiest of my three births.

Despite the excitement and confusion, we were conscious of God's Divine hand guiding us, protecting us, and accommodating us. My husband and I appeared so calm and composed the hospital staff did not realize that I was on the brink of giving birth in their hallway. That's what happens when you tap into the strength of Jesus; He fills you with tranquility and peace – regardless of your circumstances, and you have the courage to do things you never imagined possible. Ephesians 2:14 reminds believers, *"For He Himself is our peace."*

Pray that God will give you the strength you need for the challenges you are facing, and remember *"…each will be rewarded according to his own labor."* (1 Corinthians 3:8). When you receive His blessings and experience His peace, keep in mind others who are still in the birthing process, and pray for them, too.

Dinner

"…they will rest from their labor, for their deeds will follow them."
(Revelation 14:13b)

⚜ **Daily Bread** – Read: 2 Corinthians 12:9

After my quick delivery, the doctor mentioned that many women in the hospital had been laboring for hours. So, I took a few moments to pray for them, asking God to provide them with needed strength to endure their momentary hardship; I prayed that they would persevere patiently, fixing their minds on the incredible joy to come.

Sometimes, when relief washes over us after a difficult trial, we tend to quickly forget the excruciating pain we just experienced. If it were not so, I don't think I would have even considered giving birth again after my first labor and delivery! I'm sure many other women feel the same way. Time heals all wounds, as the old saying goes. The apostle Paul reminded believers to shed the past and move forward: *"…Forgetting what is behind and straining toward what is ahead, I press on toward the goal to win the prize for which God has called me heavenward in Christ Jesus."* (Philippians 3:13b-14).

As another day ends, and your stomach continues to growl, pray for those who are truly enduring pain: in childbirth, in childlessness, or through any other physical or emotional trauma. Ask the Lord to give them comfort in His Word: *"But those who suffer He delivers in their suffering; He speaks to them in their affliction."* (Job 36:15).

DAY 24
Affliction

Breakfast

*"What a friend we have in Jesus, all our sins and griefs to bear!
What a privilege to carry everything to God in prayer!"
– Hymn by Joseph M. Scriven, circa 1855*

⚜ Daily Bread – Read: Psalm 119:67-72

"Today I am celebrating that with which the Lord has been filling me: a desire to know Him better, a hunger for more of Him, and a better understanding of Who He is and how I can be more like Him – especially in the way He acts towards others. I don't want to act like Jesus in order to feel better about myself. I genuinely want to be a better person and do a better job of helping and caring for others. How quickly my thoughts go to myself – the pain in my head and the exhaustion I feel. I just want to sleep; I am so tired. I see everyone eat the food that I prepare, and I just want to stuff my mouth – not because I'm even the least bit hungry but just for the flavor of something better than my own saliva. My throat is sore, so I think I will just have some juice." (My Fasting Journal, Day 24).

How frighteningly easy it is to give up and give in to our emotions right on the heels of a victory. How quickly our giant steps forward can backtrack! In today's Daily Bread Scripture reading, King David recognized that his own affliction led him to obedience in the Lord. In the midst of pain, our first fleshly impulse is to turn on our heels and flee in the opposite direction, but our immediate and singular saintly solution should be to run straight into the arms of Jesus. Isaiah 49:13b reminds, *"For the LORD comforts His people and will have compassion on His afflicted ones."*

Through fasting, you learn to stay the course, press in through the pain, and watch God at work. You see His comfort – not only in your own life but also in the lives of others for whom you've prayed. Each day, your walk takes you closer and closer to Him, and you see Him not only as your Father but also as your Faithful Friend, walking right beside you each step of the way. He's close by your side: guiding the way, holding your hand, and catching you when you fall. Proverbs 18:24b refers to God as *"a friend who sticks closer than a brother"*.

For whom can you be that kind of friend? It's one thing to pray for them, but it's quite another to actively serve as the hands and feet of Jesus. Are you willing to put your prayers into action today? Pray, and then follow His lead.

_____
_____
_____

Broken and Weak ⚜ 93

Lunch

"And let us consider how we may spur one another on toward love and good deeds."
(Hebrews 10:24)

⚜ **Daily Bread** – Read: Psalm 119:33-34

Obedience to God means knowing His will and following His ways. The more time I have spent in His Word, the more He has nourished my soul. In Jeremiah 29:13 the Lord promises, *"You will seek Me and find Me when you seek Me with all your heart."*

When you truly desire to know Him, He opens your eyes, sharpens your mind, and softens your heart. He has frequently and graciously provided me fresh insight to Scriptures that I have read many times before, and He has often led me to specific passages to share with friends. God confirms His Will with His Word, and with the people He brings into your life. In this way, He reassures you that you are correctly sensing His direction and following the right path.

I always pray, silently, as friends share their burdens with me, and I ask the Lord to lead me to the Scriptures that will best comfort or encourage them. Think of the people whom God has introduced to you during your fast; their presence in your life is not coincidental. Ask the Lord what Scriptures would be good confirmation for their particular needs. Then, e-mail them, phone them, or send them a card. You'll be surprised and delighted to hear back from many of them when they later share that your encouragement was perfectly timed and just what they needed.

There is no better gift to give a friend than the perfectly chosen Word of God. Study it daily; memorize it. Write down what the Lord presses upon your heart, and share it with others.

Dinner

"When people pray, the enemy hasn't much chance to come in between while the Holy Spirit works."
— Corrie ten Boom

⚜ **Daily Bread** – Read: James 4:7-10

When Jesus fasted in the desert, He used the Scriptures as His weapon of choice to deflect the enemy's deceitful advances. The enemy will attack you, too, especially during your fast, and, often, in his effort to wound you, he will twist things all around, attacking those whom you love and attacking you through them. The enemy knows that, as you grow in your relationship with the Lord, your relationship with others will be restored, and he hates both of those scenarios. The enemy is a bully; he doesn't fight fair, and he purposefully hits below the belt. He abhors peace and despises harmony but delights in creating chaos and confusion.

Diligently pray for Divine protection to shield you and those in your life. Recognize the enemy's temptations from the Lord's tests, and remember Lamentations 3:33: *"For He does not willingly bring affliction or grief to the children of men."*

"Be self-controlled and alert. Your enemy the devil prowls around like a roaring lion looking for someone to devour. Resist him, standing firm in the faith, because you know that your brothers throughout the world are undergoing the same kind of sufferings." (1 Peter 5:8-9). In a nutshell, this means that we must know the Word of God.

"For the Word of God is living and active. Sharper than any double-edged sword …" (Hebrews 4:12a). Dedicate yourself to becoming thoroughly familiar with the Sword of the Spirit, God's True Word. Then, you will recognize the enemy's fraudulent use of it, and you can confidently and swiftly fight fire with Fire. Tonight, pray that all believers will do the same.

DAY 25

Weak and Weary

Breakfast

"He gives strength to the weary and increases the power of the weak."
(Isaiah 40:29)

⚜ **Daily Bread** – Read: Isaiah 50:4-5

"This morning, I took the kids to a play up north; it was a long drive there and back. Once home, we barely had time for my daughter to change into her dance clothes before joining the southbound traffic and driving to her dance studio. I really wanted to break down and cry on the drive to her dance class. My husband suggested that I stay in the van, and take a nap during her class. But, I had brought my Bible and my current Bible study, and I really felt I just needed a good meal with the Lord. I knew from the experience of the past few weeks that His Word does more to give me energy and strength than any nap ever could." (My Fasting Journal, Day 25).

His Word is the Bread of Life. By making time, even (and especially!) in our most weary state, we will be filled with sustenance from the Scriptures as the power of His Word flows through us. What an amazing feeling to be on the receiving end of those rations! It's even more incredible to realize that the Lord will feed everyone that way if only we stop to receive it.

Nothing surpasses the power of God's Word. In testimony after testimony, fellow believers have shared modern day miracles from the restoration of broken marriages to the redemption of desecrated lives. Our God is the God of the impossible, and He accomplishes much of it today through the power of His written Word.

"Let the Word of Christ dwell in you richly …", urges Colossians 3:16a. This morning, be filled as you read and study His Word. When your strength begins to fade, rejuvenate yourself with a big serving of Scripture. You can even have seconds! And, as James 1:22 directs, *"Do not merely listen to the Word and so deceive yourselves. Do what it says."*

What particular Scriptures speak to you? Do you have them memorized?

_____
_____
_____
_____
_____

Lunch

"Like newborn babies, crave pure spiritual milk, so that by it you may grow up in your salvation, now that you have tasted that the Lord is good."
(1 Peter 2:2-3)

⚜ **Daily Bread** – Read: Mark 1:35-39

Your energy is rapidly draining; it's time for a refill! Open your Bible and enjoy a lunch that is sweeter than milk and honey. *"How sweet are your words to my taste, sweeter than honey to my mouth!"* (Psalm 119:103).

I have been known to have an overactive sweet tooth, and before I began my 40-day fast, I literally could not make it through the day without the taste of chocolate in my mouth. I was addicted. I love sweets (although I am not a big fan of honey!), and today, I can say that I have found something sweeter than chocolate – the Word of God.

My cravings for chocolate and other sweets have dwindled significantly; one of my personal prayers during my fast was to eat more healthfully. I am grateful for the sweet substitute that the Lord provided me (and I don't mean Splenda®!). When we're weak and weary, there are so many options available for an energy boost. For me, it was a cheap chocolate fix. For Jesus, it was beneficial and wholesome refreshment from His Father. *"Very early in the morning, while it was still dark, Jesus got up, left the house and went off to a solitary place, where He prayed."* (Mark 1:35).

At this point in the Bible story, Jesus had chosen His disciples; He was teaching, healing, and driving out evil spirits. If anyone was truly weary, it must have been Him! But, instead of sleeping in the next morning, He woke up even earlier to pray and to be alone with His Heavenly Father. He knew the source of His strength, and He wasted no time in tapping it. The Father gave Jesus – and gives us – not only strength but also direction. Because of our limited earthly vision, God must continually reorient us to His great Kingdom plan.

After Jesus renewed His strength and received Divine direction, He packed up and moved on to the next village. There were still many people who needed help right there where He was; He could have easily pitched a tent, made Himself at home, and continued His ministry without the hassle of moving on to another unfamiliar place. But, meeting with His Father kept Jesus focused on God's Will. And, the Father planned for Jesus to cover as much ground as possible in the very short time He had on earth. Eternity was at stake; it was time to move forward, and Jesus obediently followed His Father's direction.

As you pray for needed strength to energize you until dinner, pray also for the Lord's direction. Be ready and willing to go where He leads.

Dinner

"Carry each other's burdens, and in this way you will fulfill the law of Christ."
(Galatians 6:2)

⚜ **Daily Bread** – Read: Galatians 6:9

God's strength benefits you as well as others through you. In Him, you become fortified to minister to many needy people around you, yet, you may believe you have no stamina to help others when you feel so weak yourself.

Through your own weakness, you better understand the deficiencies of others. When your own strength is tenuous, you must determine to persevere despite your human shortcomings and through the sheer power of God. As you fast, your weakness is a choice; you rely on God and take Him at His Word to help you endure. Jesus reprimanded His disciples in Gethsemane, *"The spirit is willing, but the body is weak."* (Matthew 26:41b). We are weak, but He is strong. Paul, explaining that human weakness is the ideal way to channel Divine power, phrased it this way in 2 Corinthians 12:10b: *"For when I am weak, then I am strong."*

Many people, though, are experiencing weakness that is out of their control and beyond their understanding. In Acts 20:35, Paul encourages the Ephesian elders, *"In everything I did, I showed you that by this kind of hard work, we must help the weak, remembering the Words the Lord Jesus Himself said: 'It is more blessed to give than to receive.'"*

Tonight, think of others whom you can bless in your weakness and through His strength. Take the power you are gaining from spending time with the Lord, and transfer it to another weak and weary traveler in need of an exhilarating pick-me-up.

DAY 26

In the Master's Hands

Breakfast

"Man looks at the outward appearance, but the LORD looks at the heart."
(1 Samuel 16:7c)

♣ Daily Bread – Read: Isaiah 64:8

When we see a chip in a cup or a crack in a plate, we determine that the item is useless and of little value. God, however, finds great worth in things that most of us just toss aside. Be thankful that He does, or most of us would be in the trash heap! It is incomprehensible that God could ever find anything serviceable amidst our damaged parts and fractured emotions, but the point we see as the end of road, God views as a starting place.

When you are broken, you fit perfectly in the nail-scarred hands of Jesus. When you stop trying to glue yourself back together and give the fragmented, sharp-edged shards of your shattered life to the King, He will create a masterpiece. He is not horrified or overwhelmed by the jigsaw puzzle that is your life…even if you're missing a piece or two. Your unfinished mess softens His heart and inspires His best work, when you humbly relinquish it to Him. The more broken, bruised, and battered you are, the better. His mind is always creating and imagining. His plans never cease, and His purposes are always magnificent.

In the Hands of the Master Potter, a hard and formless lump of clay is molded into a perfect vessel. In the Hands of the Master Carpenter, a rough, splintered, wooden life is smoothed until it is serviceable and beautiful, bearing no resemblance to its former unwieldy state. In the Hands of the Master Architect and Builder, a crude map bearing the erasures of many mistakes and wrong turns, becomes an intricate and perfectly designed blueprint in His Kingdom plan. The Master Creator will only work with what is surrendered to Him, but what He will do with a life released into His care is inconceivable.

The world expects – and demands – independence and self-sufficiency. But, human beings have limits, and, in some way, we will always fall short. Isn't there always someone who is stronger, faster, smarter, richer, better looking, or more talented? Luke 16:15 reminds us, *"…God knows your hearts. What is highly valued among men is detestable in God's sight."* Self-made men and women are admired and emulated in the distorted human mind, but, then, haven't we established that the world is not all its cracked up to be? Oh, it's cracked up all right, leading us right back full circle to the very reason we must surrender ourselves to God: so He can put us all back together again.

This morning, acknowledge the Great Restorer, and tell Him you're sick and tired of being sick and tired. Pile your broken pieces in a heap at His feet; He will gather them all in His loving hands, and restore you into a beautiful, wonderful, purposeful being - a royal child of the Most High King.

Lunch

"God does not have problems, only plans."
— Corrie ten Boom

⚜ **Daily Bread** — Read: Jeremiah 18:6-10

It's difficult to comprehend that God wants our garbage. Yet, He does — every last stinking shred of it. The shells of our helpless, hopeless, lifeless forms hang like worn out rag dolls in His big, strong, gentle, merciful Hands.

The world requires Ivy League educations, achievement-laden resumes, and personal goal-oriented plans; no others need apply. God's door, however, is open wide, announcing, *"All Others Welcome Here"*. He did not design His children for this world, so we do not have to conform to its formidable expectations and demanding standards. He instructs us in 1 John 2:15, *"Do not love the world or anything in the world."* As far as principles go, God's bar is set so high, we can't reach it no matter how hard we try or how diligently we prepare. Praise Him that Jesus bridges the gap for us!

God does not want His children assimilating to this world; our choice to do so grieves Him greatly. Why do we want to live a life for which He already died? As Jesus said to His disciples in Matthew 16:26, *"What good will it be for a man if he gains the whole world, yet forfeits his soul?"* Our sins and shortcomings were crucified at Calvary; we're to leave them at the foot of cross — not pick them up and drag them around with us. All we're to take away is the new life He gave us, and it does not include the bedraggled, travel-worn baggage from our former existence. Lighten your load! There will be more room for the Holy Spirit to fill you, more time to study His Holy Word, and more ease in dropping to your knees before Him.

Are you still living with one foot in the world? You can't serve two masters. And, by the way, not making a choice *is* a choice; it's a sin of omission. By failing to actively choose Him, you are casting a "No" vote in His favor, and it will reveal itself to be a sorrowful election on Judgment Day.

Are you going to eat at Burger King® or with the King of Kings? Take a look at the world's menu and compare it to God's offerings. There's no contest.

___

Dinner

"No discipline seems pleasant at the time, but painful. Later on, however, it produces a harvest of righteousness and peace for those who have been trained by it."
(Hebrews 12:11)

⚜ **Daily Bread** – Read: Romans 9:20-21

Living in this fallen world, we are constantly reminded of our inadequacies. God wired us to do more and to be more, but the enemy pits others against us (and even turns us on ourselves!) in an attempt to box us in and render us useless. Our resulting fear paralyzes us; we think, "I can't. Why try? I'm not good enough. Someone else will do it, and they'll probably do it better anyway." But, deep in our hearts, we know that we were meant for more than what the world allows. If, in our confusion and despair, we cry out to our Heavenly Father, we signal our readiness to be mightily used for His glory.

He desires that we fear Him – not to be afraid or frightened of Him, but to be in awe of and revere Him. The Bible is full of passages about fearing the Lord. "The fear of the LORD is the beginning of wisdom." (Psalm 111:10a). "…Blessed is the man who fears the LORD, who finds great delight in His commands." (Psalm 112:1). *"To fear the LORD is to hate evil…"* (Proverbs 8:13). There are many, many others. Take the time to find them through your Bible concordance, and study the meaning of the passages.

Remember the old saying, "One man's trash is another man's treasure?" Well, no matter how the world discards or discounts us, we all have the potential to be God's found treasures. In Exodus 19:5, God instructed Moses to tell the Israelites that they will be His *"treasured possession"*. That sentiment is repeated in Deuteronomy 7:6, and, in 2 Corinthians 4:7, Paul lets us know that we all "have this treasure in jars of clay" meaning that God's power and goodness resides in His believers despite our humble and unworthy appearances.

Crude and crumbling though we are, God does view us as His treasures. In His eyes, we are quite the catch, and, In His light, our ordinary use becomes extraordinary. Our new Divine luster mirrors His glory and goodness, and our resplendence is anything but commonplace.

Reflect on your current application. If it's anything less than God's best, you're selling yourself short. Romans 8:28 reminds us "…*that in all things God works for the good of those who love Him, who have been called according to His purpose.*" Humbly surrender to Him, and pray to be used for His higher and better purposes.

DAY 27
Who's In Charge

Breakfast

"…Can we find anyone like this man, one in whom is the Spirit of God?"
(Genesis 41:38)

⚜ **Daily Bread** – Read: Genesis 41:41-57

"We are studying the life of Joseph in our Bible study this week. Joseph's ministry was not in the church. He was in a position of public influence. As believers, we often feel our ministry is limited inside the church walls, so, it was really good to hear that many of us are placed in the public and secular arena to minister outside the walls of the church." (My Fasting Journal, Day 27).

Last fall, I attended a leadership conference and was really struck by the comments made by one of the speakers. He said, that as Christians, we can join Christian churches, socialize in Christian coffee shops, attend Christian schools, frequent Christian concerts, shop at Christian bookstores, wear Christian clothes, and set ourselves completely apart from the rest of the world. We have, at times, so disassociated ourselves, that we retain no interest in mingling with people who are not Christians. I don't think that is what God meant when He set us apart. In the Great Commission (Matthew 28:19), Jesus commands us to *"go and make disciples of all nations, baptizing them in the name of the Father and of the Son and of the Holy Spirit…"*. He didn't say go and hide from them!

It's sometimes easy to forget for Whom we're living. The truly victorious Christian follows the example of Jesus Christ Who walked among – not away from – the sick and the sinful. Otherwise, our concern becomes self-centered rather than God-centered. Christians can not become so immersed in doing the Lord's work amongst ourselves that we fail to extend our sphere of influence to the ones who really need it – the unsaved. It is possible to be in this world without being of this world, as Jesus prayed for us in the 17th chapter of John.

Consider where God has planted you, and how many people come across your path each day. Do you associate only with fellow believers? If so, you're missing some Divine opportunities on behalf of Christ. Ask Him to give you fresh eyes to recognize them as well as courage to initiate contact.

_____
_____
_____
_____
_____

Lunch

"Whatever you do, work at it with all your heart, as working for the Lord, not for men…"
(Colossians 3:23)

⚜ **Daily Bread** – Read: Matthew 25:21

Some of us may feel as our job has little purpose or significance in furthering God's Kingdom. The truth is that any job worth doing is worth doing well. Any work that is decent, honorable, and well-performed represents Christ.

When I was 18 years old, I had to write my personal philosophy for a business class. I wrote, "If I give my best and do my best, I'll receive the best." That is definitely true if what I'm doing is what God desires. The Lord starts out small with most of us, and He watches our faithfulness. When He sees our willingness to work, to learn, and to grow, and when He knows our obedience is in humble and earnest desire to accomplish what He has set before us, He will entrust us with greater responsibility.

Remember, though, that greater responsibility yields greater accountability. Jesus advised His disciples in Luke 12:48b: "From everyone who has been given much, much will be demanded; and from the one who has been entrusted with much, much more will be asked." That is not a burden; it's a Holy privilege!

God knows exactly what we're capable of accomplishing, and He loves to reward us with more, if we responsibly manage what little we already have, be it time, talent, or money. Today, you may be questioning why someone else got the position for which you felt best suited while you received a task seemingly below your ability. Submit your disappointment to God, and trust in His sovereign Will. No one can stand in the way of His plans and purposes for your life. Be encouraged by 1 Chronicles 29:11-12 (New Living Translation): *"Yours, O LORD, is the greatness, the power, the glory, the victory, and the majesty. Everything in the heavens and on earth is Yours, O LORD, and this is Your Kingdom. We adore You as the One Who is over all things. Wealth and honor come from You alone, for Your rule over everything. Power and might are in Your hand, and at Your discretion, people are made great and given strength."*

If He placed you in an area where you are required to wait, then wait patiently but work diligently. Glean all you can right where you are, and work with an attitude of humility and gratitude. God looks carefully at our responses to our situations and circumstances. Do you realize that for all of His faithfulness, Moses was denied entrance into the Promised Land because of one unholy temper tantrum (see Numbers 20:1-13 and Deuteronomy 32:48-52)? We can grumble, complain, and succumb to fleshly fretting, or we can get busy, remain faithful, and use our time to be good students and good teachers.

Be willing to serve wherever the Lord places you, in whatever capacity He chooses. Pray that you learn all that He intends for you to receive in your present position so that you will be ready for the next assignment. Remember, Joseph went from chafing chains to royal robes, and from caring for prisoners to caring for a country. You do not want to be ill-prepared for the next job God has for you. Pray that He will grant you awareness and discernment so you can recognize the reason why you're in your current position. Value your time there as God tutors you for your next mission.

Dinner

"If anyone would come after me, he must deny himself and take up his cross daily and follow me."
(Luke 9:23)

🌿 **Daily Bread** – Read: Acts 17:24-28

God controls everything. He created everything. He designed us to follow Him, and He puts us in charge as He sees fit.

We often struggle between doing our own thing and doing the Will of our Father. Sometimes, we try to separate our spiritual life from our vocational life, but we are gravely mistaken if we think we can compartmentalize God Almighty. He will not be put on a shelf, shoved in a corner, or hidden in a box until we are ready to see Him again. He is in all things – without segregation.

There is nothing God needs from us, but He loves us and desires to have a relationship with us. Our obedience pleases Him; it shows our respect for His authority. When we thankfully acknowledge that He is in charge, He mercifully receives our reverence. Like any good parent, our Heavenly Father wants to bless us and show us the respect that we show Him. His love for us is not dependent upon our love for Him, but He does love to bless our obedience as exemplified throughout the Bible including Deuteronomy 7:12-15.

Is any part of your life off limits God? What you're gripping in your hand can not be held in His. What you're hiding in a closet can not be unleashed for the Kingdom's glory. Be obedient. Surrender. He knows what you're holding and hiding anyway, and He wants to free you from its burden. Confess your control issues to your Father; you'll be relieved by the lightened load!

DAY 28

Foot Washing

Breakfast

"But be very careful to keep the commandment and the law that Moses the servant of the LORD gave you: to love the LORD your God, to walk in all His ways, obey His commands, to hold fast to Him and to serve Him with all your heart and all your soul."
(Joshua 22:5)

⚜ **Daily Bread** – Read: John 13:3-5

"Jesus knew that the time had come for Him to leave this world and go to the Father. Having loved His own who were in the world, He now showed them the full extent of His love." (John 13:1).

The thirteenth chapter of John is one of my favorites in the Bible because of the words you just read. Jesus loved His followers so much, and yet He knew He had to physically leave them. As a parent, I can barely imagine the prospect of leaving my young and vulnerable children alone to fend for themselves. If you knew you were leaving, wouldn't you want to cherish every single moment you had left with your children and do everything possible to prepare them for your departure? Ever aware that they didn't really understand why you were leaving them, wouldn't you set everything else aside, spend time alone with them, and love them the best way you knew how during the time you had left?

For Jesus, "the full extent of His love" was illustrated in humble service through the most menial of tasks. He knew that the path His disciples would travel next would be more dangerous and difficult that the road they had traveled so far. They would need to stand firm, walk in peace, and serve as leaders for the next followers of Christ. His were extremely big sandals to fill!

Jesus came to cleanse our entire bodies; washing the feet of the disciples symbolized the spiritual cleansing that would wash away the sins of everyone who accepted the blood He shed on the cross. His lesson in humility provided a principle of selfless service for His original disciples as well as for His modern-day disciples; it prepared the twelve to function without His physical presence just as it instructs us today. Before you step foot in the world this morning, ask God to prepare you to walk in peace and to humbly live as He exemplified.

_____
_____
_____
_____

Lunch

"I have set you an example that you should do as I have done for you."
(John 13:15)

⚜ **Daily Bread** – Read: 1 John 3:1-3, 5:1-5

Children are dear to Jesus' heart. Everyone on earth is God's creation although not everyone has chosen to be a part of His family. *"He was in the world,"* states John 1:10-13, *"and though the world was made through Him, the world did not recognize Him. He came to that which was His own, but His own did not receive Him. Yet to all who received Him, to those who believed in His name, He gave the right to become children of God – children born not of natural descent, nor of human decision or a husband's will, but born of God."* As believers, we are His precious children, and we never grow out of our need for Him.

If Jesus grieved leaving His children behind, I imagine He is rightly appalled at the number of earthly children who are abandoned and left behind on a daily basis in our sin-filled world. The number of children who are killed and discarded is an atrocity, and one that the Lord will judge with a vengeance. In the first three gospels, Jesus directs, *"Let the little children come to me, and do not hinder them, for the Kingdom of Heaven belongs to such as these."* (Matthew 19:14; see also Mark 10:14 and Luke 18:16).

Desiring that none should perish, He Himself arrived as a baby in human flesh to cleanse our dirty hearts and fill our empty lives, and He expects His children to emulate His example of humble service and sacrificial life. We are to care for another – physically, emotionally, and spiritually – as He cared, and continues to care, for us.

During your fast, you've experienced some of the weakness that Jesus Himself suffered during His 40 days in the desert. Beyond that, though, you've encountered the realization that something more is at stake, and Someone else is important than your own comfort and convenience. That Someone requires us to think less of ourselves and more of others.

Jesus' time in the desert confirmed that nothing – and no one – would hinder His Father's will. He leads you now to deny yourself and to follow Him, wherever He leads and whatever the sacrifice. *"…You are a chosen people,"* the apostle Peter tells us in 1 Peter 2:9, *"a royal priesthood, a holy nation, a people belonging to God, that you may declare the praises of Him Who called you out of darkness into His wonderful light."*

How can you show His love to, and shed His light on, those He has, by no coincidence, placed in your life?

Dinner

"God uses our problems as building materials for His miracles."
— Corrie ten Boom, Tramp for the Lord

⚜ Daily Bread – Read: Luke 7:44-47

The disciples had the presence of Jesus in physical form; God, in human flesh, was leading them as He lived among them. They saw His miracles; they were aware of His power, yet when He asked them to feed the crowd of five thousand, they considered the task to be preposterous. Isn't it laughable that the disciples could stand right beside the Creator of the world and still doubt His omnipotence? Sadly, we do the same thing all the time.

Although we do not see Jesus physically as the disciples did, evidence of His power and majesty blankets all of creation from small, miraculous everyday moments to enormous, life-transforming testimonies. When Jesus commands us to do something, regardless of how overwhelming it may seem to us, He's not bluffing but neither is He tricking us. He doesn't expect us to complete the task through our own limited power, but He does quietly measure our response. He watches for obedience in spite of limited resources, for faith in the presence of obstacles, for trust in the absence of information. Will we persevere through our human fears and doubts, and choose to fully rely on Him for provision and guidance, or will we balk like stubborn mules, refusing to take another step until we know the exact details of the plan and the exact route of the journey?

Matthew 20:28 reminds us that the Son of Man, Jesus Christ, came to serve, not to be served, and He tells us in Luke 12:35 to be dressed and ready for service ourselves. We can not do much through our own power, but we can do all things through Him who strengthens us! (Philippians 4:13). Every day abounds with ordinary opportunities for service requiring God-sized abilities of performance. Pray for open eyes to see such circumstances, for a proper spirit to discern them, and for a willing heart to act upon them, in the name – and for the glory – of Jesus Christ.

Broken and Weak ⚜ 109

5
Finding Rest

"Come to Me, all you who are weary and burdened, and I will give you rest. Take My yoke upon you and learn from Me, for I am gentle and humble in heart, and you will find rest for your souls. For My yoke is easy and My burden is light."
(Matthew 11:28-30)

You've been through so much this month; can you believe you're nearing the finish line? If you've persevered through the full 40-day fast, you're now entering a unique and welcome stage – a place of rest. Odd as it seems in the midst of life's hurry and scurry, God specifically creates time for you to rest after you've endured a difficult time. In this time of fasting, you've been broken and emptied; you know you've been well-used, but you still feel used up. With hardly anything left to give, you've learned to serve in your weakness. Now, God will give you rest in response to your work and in preparation for your future assignments.

Service may be crucial, but rest is also essential in the proper balance. In the Old Testament, God even gave the land a rest: In Leviticus 25:4, He commanded that, every seventh year, the land was to receive a year of rest from its crops; in Joshua 14:15, He rested the land from war. And, of course, He Himself rested from His work on the seventh day after creating the heavens and the earth (Genesis 2:2). Jesus, too, knew the importance of rest, and made sure that in the midst of His ministry, He rested in His Father as exemplified in Matthew 14:13 & 23.

The interesting thing about God's rest is that it requires action. He doesn't tell you to relax by napping, or to rest by sleeping. He says, *"Take My yoke upon you and learn from Me."* Your rest is not mindless idleness but a peaceful, soul-restoring time of reflection and further instruction. The rest He offers is not so much for your weary physical body; He has a glorious resurrected body designed for you when your earthly one is worn out. His rest is for your soul. *"My soul finds rest in God alone…"* David proclaims in Psalm 62:1. The Lord says in Jeremiah 6:16 that if you walk in the good and godly paths of Judah's ancestors, "you will find rest for your souls."

When we pass from these temporary dwellings to our heavenly homes, our souls go with us. So, why do we spend so much time neglecting them while perfecting our outward appearances and physical bodies? Your soul is the true essence of your being. The soul clings to God (Psalm 63:8); the soul experiences joy (Psalm 94:19); the soul praises God (Psalm 103:1); the soul is saddened (Psalm 42:11); the soul can not be killed by man (Matthew 10:28). Praise God for His mercy outlined in the 23rd Psalm: *"…He makes me lie down in green pastures, He leads me beside quiet waters, He restores my soul."*

Your soul needs rest, and during this God-provided sabbatical, He is calling a Divine time-out so that you can learn from Him and grow in Him. Do not remain weary; do not lose heart. This time of rest is for your benefit. God is calling you to a higher purpose. Bigger responsibilities are ahead for those who have been faithful in small matters. Rest and preparation precede further action; you must step only on the ground the

Lord has placed before you. Do not get ahead of Him, and do not fall behind Him. Rest in Him for now, and you will be ready for your next anointed assignment.

Much ground remains uncovered; many lives exist untouched. God is constantly searching for the faithful few who will follow Him, believe Him, trust Him, and allow Him to work through them. *"Humble yourselves, therefore, under God's mighty hand, that He may lift you up in due time. Cast all your anxiety on Him because He cares for you."* (1 Peter 5:6-7). Be willing to stand in the gap for Jesus.

Until that time, rest well, beloved. Do not fall asleep, but be watchful and alert as you remain at the Father's table and continue your bountiful feast!

DAY 29

Sunset

Breakfast

"So that from the rising of the sun to the place of its setting men may know there is none beside Me. I am the LORD, and there is no other."
(Isaiah 45:6)

⚜ **Daily Bread** – Read: Psalm 66:1-4

I recently accompanied my husband on his business trip to southern California. I went purely for relaxation as well as for the opportunity to enjoy the sunshine. Unfortunately, the first two days of our visit were overcast and cool, and I had not packed for that kind of weather. In our hotel room, I perused a local travel magazine and read an article detailing the top ten things to do while in the area.

We once lived in California and had our share of out-of-state guests whom we ferried to all of the touristy hot spots including Rodeo Drive, Hollywood, Walk of Fame, and Knotts Berry Farm, and I expected the article I read to include these popular sites. Surprisingly, eight of the ten recommendations revolved around enjoying the beauty and simplicity of God's creation. That's not what they were called in the magazine article, but that's exactly what they were: beautiful parks, botanical gardens, and mountain excursions. The number one suggestion on the list was to "watch the sunset on the beach".

Millions of people spend tens of thousands of dollars to vacation in sunny California, and the most recommended activity is something that most of us can enjoy from our own backyards. I found it wonderfully satisfying that the secular magazine paid homage to God's extraordinary creations (whether or not the editors and writers realized it!). A travel magazine suggested bypassing the attractions and distractions, and exiting the crowds and rush hour traffic to sit back and soak in the beauty of a sunset. If the world can acknowledge the importance of resting and enjoying the simple pleasures in life, then we should certainly honor our Creator by tuning out the busy man-made productions and tuning in the simply majestic God-created masterpieces.

Take time this morning to rest in God's goodness and reflect on the fact that, out of all His glorious creations, you are the most significant and beautiful in His eyes. Now, that's an awesome wonder!

_____
_____
_____
_____

Lunch

"For since the creation of the world God's invisible qualities – His eternal power and Divine nature – have been clearly seen, being understood from what has been made, so that men are without excuse."
(Romans 1:20)

⚜ **Daily Bread** – Read: Ecclesiastes 3:11-14

My mother visited recently, and she brought a paper that I wrote in the ninth grade entitled "The Sunset". It was a creative writing assignment that received high marks and high praise from my teacher. While I forgot that I had written the paper, I remembered the difficult year in which I wrote it.

That period of time had been marked with instability in my parents' marriage, and I had experienced a very real teenage awkwardness and faintheartedness that made me more introverted than I already was. How I let my mind escape to such a beautiful place and how I composed such eloquent words in the midst of my turmoil and anxiety astounds me now, in retrospect.

Deep within our souls, God has placed the wonder and awe of Who He is. No matter how hard the world presses in or pulls at us, God is always planted inside, giving us opportunity to catch a glimpse of Him in our reflection.

Today, praise Him for all the ways He shows Himself to you, and thank Him for the ways He reveals Himself in the depths of your difficulties. Our darkness can not hide His beauty.

Dinner

"But his delight is in the law of the LORD, and on His law he meditates day and night."
(Psalm 1:2)

⚜ **Daily Bread** – Read: Luke 6:12

I really look forward to the end of each day, when all my children are asleep in their beds, and I can have some quiet time to myself with no interruptions. Even as the sunset transitions the world into darkness, there is peaceful comfort in knowing that the day is ending, and the world is at rest.

Twilight is the perfect opportunity to record the day's events and to spend time in prayer, as Jesus did in our Daily Bread scripture. By ending the day in Him, we sleep in perfect slumber with restful and holy thoughts.

Through your fasting, God reveals Himself with greater clarity; your eyes seem sharper to see Him; your ears seem stronger to hear Him; your mind seems clearer to discern Him. But, the vast majority of the population is running around, taking care of business, completely oblivious to His presence.

Tonight, before you go to bed, spend some time journaling. Take time to reflect on God's wonderful creation, and the work that He has given you within it. Pray for those around you who are so distracted by life that they fail to live, missing the splendor of His majesty in the process.

_____
_____
_____
_____
_____
_____
_____
_____
_____
_____
_____
_____
_____
_____
_____
_____
_____
_____
_____
_____
_____
_____
_____

DAY 30
Taste and See

Breakfast

"If you try to analyze it (the Bible) as a book of science or even a book of theology, you can not be nourished by it. Like chocolate, it is to be eaten and enjoyed, not picked apart bit by bit."
— Corrie ten Boom

♧ Daily Bread – Read: Psalm 34:8-10

"Yuck! I did not wake up with a good taste in my mouth. Thirty days and counting, and I thought I had lost my taste for everything, but, this morning, my tongue felt weird. When I went to the bathroom mirror, I was grossed out when I saw that my tongue was completely covered in white. Why hadn't I noticed this before? Upon closer examination, I discovered that the whiteness was, in fact, hundreds of tiny spores. My taste buds had risen up like tiny little protestors signaling their rebellion: 'Feed us now! We are dying! We demand our right to eat again!' I was disgusted!" (My Fasting Journal, Day 30).

The initial pain and hunger during my fast was one thing; the waste eliminating from my body was quite another. The weight loss warranted no complaints, but this? I wasn't sure if my taste buds had actually died or if they could ever be revived. I debated whether or not my husband should see my whitewashed tongue for fear that he might not ever want to kiss me again!

I realized that my carpeted tongue was becoming a distraction, and I could choose to deal with it in one of two ways. I could give into my distress about my tormented taste buds and believe the enemy's lie that my tongue would die if I didn't start eating right away, or I could surrender my distress to God and pray that He would protect me and restore my tongue to its normal state when my fast was complete. I decided to taste some fresh juice, swallow the refreshing Word of God, and remain focused.

Are you also experiencing physical rebellions indicating that your body is not very supportive of your spirit's desire to be obedient to God? You've only got ten more days to go, and you're getting closer to where God wants you to be. Press in today, and drink in His Holy Word. Pray that you remain focused and do not miss what He has to show you this morning.

_____
_____
_____
_____
_____

Lunch

*"For the kingdom of God is not a matter of eating and drinking,
but of righteousness, peace and joy in the Holy Spirit…"*
(Romans 14:17)

⚜ **Daily Bread** – Read: Romans 14:19-21

The bad taste in my mouth made me think of the awful things that sometimes come out of my mouth. Occasionally, we just need to keep our mouths shut because what we say in anger, in arrogance, or in ignorance often puts a terrible taste in someone else's mouth.

Our words should be edifying and encouraging; they should build others up, not tear them down. We need forgiveness for the fleshy and impulsive words we sometimes choose as well as forgiveness for failing to speak more of God's Holy and thoughtful Word. And, don't forget to use the power of God's Word to make the enemy flee! Remember that *"the Word of God is living and active. Sharper than any double-edged sword, it penetrates even to dividing soul and spirit, joints and marrow; it judges the thoughts and attitudes of the heart."* (Hebrews 4:12).

Choose to memorize some morsels from God's Word today; they will freshen your breath with His Truth and extinguish the bad aftertaste of the enemy's filthy and deceptive language. Ask the Lord to forgive your negative, critical taunts and to replace them with the eloquence of His loving words of wisdom. Pray for those in your life who need encouragement, and choose to articulate an expression of Christ.

Dinner

"A word aptly spoken is like apples of gold in settings of silver."
(Proverbs 25:11)

⚜ **Daily Bread** – Read: Psalm 119:97-104

Although it's odd to think of words tasting good, I've found that replacing my meals with time in the Scriptures is actually more enjoyable than any food I've ever eaten. The Bread of Life better sustains me, further increases my desire, and completely nourishes me in a way that physical food can not.

Traditional meals serve only to maintain our physical bodies, but the Word of God feeds our minds, hearts, and souls. It yields encouragement which we can boldly share; it provides ammunition to protect us against enemy attacks. It speaks truth; it edifies us; it sustains us. It overflows from our hearts and through our mouths. When put into action, God's Truth becomes evident in our lives; we walk in assurance, confidence, and courage. We radiate peace and exude joy, affecting all with whom we come in contact.

No physical food offers what spiritual food supplies. Thank the Lord for His amply supply of your Daily Bread. How has your spiritual dinner replenished you tonight?

DAY 31

Holy Hunger

Breakfast

"Blessed are those who hunger and thirst for righteousness, for they will be filled."
(Matthew 5:6)

⚜ **Daily Bread** – Read: Psalm 100

This morning, as you sit down to breakfast with the Lord, consider what an awesome privilege it is to dine with the Creator of all! He chose you long before you chose Him.

You are nearing the end of your fast; you will soon be breaking it. But, actually, that's what you do every morning. After a night of sleep and rest, you "break fast" and start the day with breakfast. And, before your day begins, dawn breaks. Something must be broken before something new begins. That is exactly what is happening to you during this fast. The hardened walls of your outer shell are breaking, and God is unveiling the new, improved you underneath.

Isn't that what God has accomplished during these past five weeks? Hasn't He broken through your tough veneer and tenderly uncovered the areas of your life that weren't fully committed to Him? Is the demolition complete? Do you like what you see? Do you think it's what He sees?

What God beholds is an image of Himself hidden inside a jar of clay. He sees the beauty and wonder of you, His intentional creation, trapped inside a fortress of your own construction, and He wants to break you out.

This week, you've reached a place of reflection. You can see the places He's broken through, crumbled down, and chipped away. You can also better recognize the barriers you're still trying to hold erect. But, you know that you've grown in your devotion to the Lord and in your desire to be with Him, and you've learned that you can't get through a single meal without Him.

Are you anticipating the day when you will finally break this fast, or, as the result of the precious time you're sharing with your Lord, are you praying that it will never end? Praise Him that the things that never break are His promises. He is always faithful.

_____
_____
_____

Lunch

"Open wide your mouth and I will fill it."
(Psalm 81:10b)

✣ **Daily Bread** – Read: 1 Peter 1:15-16

In his book, *Knowing God Through Fasting*, Elmer Towns wrote, "Fasting is holy poverty. You don't fast to make yourself weak, but to build character. Fasting is holy hunger, not to make you famished, but to make you holy."

Spiritual hunger is just that. It's a longing, a craving that you just can't seem to satisfy. It's a desire to know God so intimately that you can't get enough of Him or His Word. Has your appetite increased for more of Him and His Daily Bread? Are you craving meal time with Him? At this point in my fast, I loved sitting at the table of the Lord, and I savored every morsel He fed me. I didn't have to clear the table or do the dishes; I just enjoyed the Company at my table.

As the Lord guided me through His Word, He introduced me to many faithful followers who dined with Him in the past. We banqueted with Paul who taught me to see things through new eyes. We dined with Job who showed me the importance of persevering through intense trials. We sat with the ever industrious Martha; she made me realize my own tendency to stay busy with earnest but not necessarily Divine tasks. Esther inspired me with the story of her own fast and her prevailing courage. The widow of Zarephath reminded me that God sustained her, too. I cried with Jonah as I remembered my own "belly of the whale" experience. My dining companions included countless others whose stories I have enjoyed and through whom I have gained the courage to tell my own account.

You and I have a lot in common with these dinner guests. They set the pace; they set the example; they were less than perfect but more than faithful. Through the God-inspired records of their lives, we are fed. Without those faithfully transcribed chronicles, our plates would be empty.

The Lord has fed many; none who have sought His sustenance have come away empty-handed. They were filled to capacity with an abundance to share. Pray that your hunger for Jesus is not a selfish one, and that your pangs are the result of a benevolent longing to share Him with others. Take time to record your own story; there's no telling who may be nourished by it.

Dinner

*"When your words came I ate them; they were my joy and my hearts delight,
for I bear your name, O Lord God Almighty."*
(Jeremiah 15:16)

🕆 **Daily Bread** – Read: Esther 4:12-16

The practice of fasting is said to have originated in the Old Testament as an act of self-denial during a time of danger or threat. In Esther's lifetime, the Jews' lives were being threatened, and Mordecai suggested that Esther plead their case before the King. Such a stand required a tremendous amount of bravery, so Esther asked the Jews in Susa to join her and her maids in a three-day fast. Through the time of fasting, accompanied by prayer, the Lord emboldened this woman with confidence to appear before the King. She placed her hope and trust in God Almighty, and He delivered.

The current and continual deterioration of our earth should alert us that danger is on the horizon. Recent earthquakes, hurricanes, and tsunamis may indicate that a bigger storm is brewing. The consistent erosion of morals and values should be an unmistakable wake-up call to all God-fearing Christians. It is time to humble ourselves, as Esther did, and pray for God's mercy on our land.

There is so much for which to pray, and I believe that God is calling us to join countless other believers to humbly fast and pray as He begins to prepare His saints for His pending return. Tonight, lift up those who are committed to fasting and praying on behalf of our country and our world. Pray that other faithful believers will join the crusade and realize the power of interceding, humbly and earnestly, for all of God's creation.

DAY 32
Seeing the Invisible

Breakfast

*"So we fix our eyes not on what is seen, but on what is unseen.
For what is seen is temporary, but what is unseen is eternal."*
(2 Corinthians 4:18)

⚜ **Daily Bread** – Read: Romans 1:18-20

Creation is tangible evidence of God's existence. Creation is His calling card; it leaves no excuse for anyone to deny His omnipotence. As recorded in this morning's Daily Bread, God's eternal power and divine nature are His invisible qualities. He calls us to submit to His power and authority, and, because His believers are indwelt with His Holy Spirit, we are able to participate in His divine nature.

While creation boasts of God's goodness and power, His nature is evidenced in the transformed lives of His children. Our renewed lives prove the reality of our unparalleled Lord! Lives change through the mercy and grace of Jesus Christ, and no one can silence the testimony or deny the metamorphosis of one who follows and believes in Him. We are set apart! *"Know that the LORD has set apart the godly for Himself."* (Psalm 4:3a).

Perhaps your vision has become clouded since you accepted Him as your Savior and Lord, or, perhaps your mind has become immune to His power and glory. Has the world distracted you from focusing on the very One who saved you? If so, take heart from these words in 1 Peter 3:15a *"…in your hearts set apart Christ as Lord."* He set us apart, and we're to set Him apart! Let that terminology sink in; we're not set aside, we're set apart! To set something aside means it is not very important. To set something apart means it is really special. Clear those scales from your eyes and see how significant you are! Shake those cobwebs from your mind and realize how magnificent He is!

If the unseeing, unsaved world has no excuse for their unbelief, imagine the accountability that we have as Christians. We were blind, but now we see! (See John 9:25). How can we effectively testify for the living Lord if we, who have seen Him who is invisible, are walking around as if we've lost our glasses?

Pray that God will renew your eyesight and restore your witness. Hindsight is 20/20 vision, as the old saying goes, but in the Kingdom of the Lord, that clarity appears too late to matter. Ask God to allow your light to shine today in the life of someone who is having trouble seeing clearly in the shadows of this dark world.

_____
_____
_____
_____
_____
_____
_____

Lunch

"Now faith is being sure of what we hope for and certain of what we do not see."
(Hebrews 11:1)

⚜ **Daily Bread** – Read: John 20:29

God blesses us for our belief. Many historical figures in the Scriptures witnessed the miracles of Jesus with their own eyes but still did not believe His deity. In fact, they questioned it. Jesus, however, knew doubt would be a difficult obstacle for us to overcome because we live in a world currently tormented by the greatest of all deceivers, the father of lies.

We please the Lord when we notice His presence and when we appreciate the many ways He shows Himself to us. So often, though, we ask Him to prove Himself to us, as if we can order up a burning bush on demand! While we're on the topic of burning bushes, and although God did reveal Himself to Moses in that way, read how Moses is described in the Hall of Faith, *"By faith …he persevered because he saw Him Who is invisible."* (Hebrews 11:27).

Your struggles may seem insurmountable; your difficulties may seem impossible. Your circumstances may cloud your vision, but God desires you to put your faith in Him. Open the Holy Bible, and pour over the testimonies of those who met Him face-to-face. Read the truth as He spoke it. Most importantly, recognize that His power exists today. His presence abounds today; His purposes flourish today; His provision overflows today.

If you've kept a journal during your fast, you are surely seeing the record of His invisible hand in your life. He is ever-present and always working. He loves to show Himself to you! God does not take pleasure in a game of hide-and-seek. In fact, every time His children have tried to hide from Him (Adam, Eve, Elijah, and Jonah, to name a few!), He is quick to call them out. He is Light, and light is revealing. He will not allow us to hide in darkness, nor will He live in the shadows. He exposes and illuminates the night, and He is our guiding light when we're afraid of the dark.

Do not fear the looming dark clouds that are trying to obscure your view of Jesus. Take courage because He is always near, leading the way and guarding your back. Find rest and comfort in the beacon of His Holy Word.

What areas of your life need to be warmed and brightened by the Lamp of God? Submit them to Him, shadows and all, and diligently seek the Scriptures which are aglow with His guidance. The Son is peeking through the clouds!

Dinner

"Faith is like radar which sees through the fog –
the reality of things at a distance that the human eye can not see."
- Corrie ten Boom, Tramp for the Lord

⚜ **Daily Bread** – Read: Colossians 1:15-16; 2 Corinthians 5:7

In my life, I have wrestled with God. He once gave me a directive, and I didn't want to obey Him because I was afraid of the people around me. My concern was not that they would hurt me; I just feared what they would think of me.

For a long time, I have been a people-pleaser. I wanted everyone to be happy and to have no unkind thoughts about me. I used to believe that if someone had a complaint against me, I must have done something wrong to warrant it. But, God has been patiently showing me, for a quite a while now, that I can not serve Him with all my heart if I am preoccupied with pleasing others. My only concern should be His delight.

Galatians 1:10 address this very issue: *"Am I now trying to win the approval of men, or of God? Or am I trying to please men? If I were still trying to please men, I would not be a servant of Christ."* We can not serve two masters, and we certainly can not please everyone all the time. So, if pleasing God becomes our first and utmost priority, He works not only in us but also through us, thereby affecting others. Ultimately, the satisfaction that others find from being around us is from God.

Nothing is more freeing than having one priority. Focusing on God alone is liberating! So often, we react to others, allowing ourselves to be pushed and pulled in a dozen different directions like puppets on a string. God is our sole touchstone, and, if we make every choice based on His direction, we can not go wrong. I have learned to submit everything to Him and to answer only to Him. My obedience has been emancipating and elating.

When I struggled with my indecision, God led me to Hebrews 11:27, and I realized that I could have as much confidence in Him as Moses did (minus the burning bush!) because I, too, see and hear the One who is invisible, and I'm paying close attention to every move He makes.

Are you lacking courage to obediently comply with God's direction in your life? Don't look to anyone else for your answers. Pray, study His Word, and ask Him to magnify His Truth. He will reveal Himself more and more with every step of faith that you take.

DAY 33

Just Breathe

Breakfast

"Breathe on me, breath of God; fill me with life anew,
that I may love what Thou dost love, and do what Thou wouldst do."
– Hymn by Edwin Hatch, circa 1878

⚜ **Daily Bread** – Read: Romans 8:9-11

Only when we place ourselves in the hands of Jesus do we truly become alive. Jesus is Life, and He gives life. Genesis 2:7 says that God's very breath is life.

I once experienced difficulty with my breathing for six months. I've never had asthma, so I had no understanding of what people endure when they can't catch their breath. My son has asthma, though, and I had seen him struggle to breathe as he ran and played.

During those six months, I suffered with costochondritis, pneumonia, and a chest wall contusion. All of these illnesses occurred one right after the other. Just as I was recovering and relearning to breathe normally, the wind was knocked out of me again.

Just taking a full breath required excessive work, and I realized how much I had taken the simple everyday act of breathing for granted. I sympathized more with my son, and, during my bout with pneumonia, my misery was shared by the entire household as we all simultaneously suffered with the same affliction.

Through my illnesses, I felt that God was trying to get my attention and enlighten me to something more than physical health. He communicated that I was to focus on things in my life that occur as naturally as breathing (or as naturally as breathing used to occur!). He revealed that I should direct my attention away from those things in my life that required unnecessary effort. He impressed upon me that if He was leading me to do something, He would give me the ability to accomplish the task. I did not have to rely on my own efforts and waste my time with a lot of futile work generated by my own power and decision. I needed to discern God's call from my own bright idea.

So often, we think that if something is not difficult, it must be worthless. A lot of people fall into the trap of believing that the way to salvation is just too easy. Believing in Jesus and accepting Him as Savior and Lord seems too elementary to some. Somehow, we think we must work harder than that to earn our eternal life. The truth is just not complicated; it is so simple that even children hear it, believe it, and accept it.

Why make things more burdensome than they are supposed to be when you can turn to Him and just breathe. Today, as you rest in Him, inhale His Holy Word, and feel the warmth of His breath as He transfuses life into your weary and overworked soul.

___

Lunch

"They are not just idle words for you – they are your life."
(Deuteronomy 32:47a)

❧ **Daily Bread** – Read: 2 Timothy 3:16-17

As believers and children of God, it ought to be quite natural for us to desire time with our Father. We should instinctively read His Word and spontaneously talk with Him throughout the day, in public and in private.

Breathing fresh air may seem routine, but when you live in a polluted, smog-filled world, the breath of God can seem like a foreign substance. The purity and holiness of Him can be a shock to our systems! However, we need to immerse ourselves in His cleanliness so that He can penetrate the dirty fog and saturate our entire beings with freshness and Truth.

Consistency is key. Do not unhook from your Divine oxygen, or you will soon be wheezing! Be relentless in your pursuit of God. Discipline yourself to study His Word, and take every opportunity to communicate with Him. Learn from those in His Holy Word who walked in righteousness with Him. Important lessons waft from their imperfect yet earnest lives, helping us learn to live and breathe in Him despite the exhaustion from this polluted world.

One day, my older daughter asked me how I became so good at cake decorating. I told her that I practiced a lot! My first cake was a disaster, but, over time, and with lots of effort, my baking became much better, and my cakes looked more beautiful. Practice makes perfect – even with something that should come as naturally as loving your Heavenly Father.

Be conscious of the air you breathe; ensure that you only inhale the highest quality. Eliminate the allergens, irritants, and toxins by filtering everything through the purity of God's Word. Breathe only the winds of encouragement and Truth, and, when your lungs are filled to capacity, live on the quality of the Breath of God. Continually practice a rhythmic respiration in Him, and you'll never be caught short-winded.

Dinner

*"You, dear children, are from God and have overcome them,
because the One Who is in you is greater than the one who is in the world."*
(1 John 4:4)

❦ **Daily Bread** – Read: Romans 12:9-21

Inhaling is vital to life, but so is exhaling. What we breathe out is as important as what we take in. If we inhale the goodness of God, we should exhale only what is pleasing and honoring to Him. Everything we say and do should express love, praise, generosity, and kindness.

In his book, *When the Enemy Strikes*, Dr. Charles Stanley stressed the importance of intentionally putting on the righteousness of Christ every single day. At one point in my walk with Christ, I found myself completely unprotected and thus exposed myself to brutal attacks from the enemy. Satan's flaming arrows exhausted even my ability to catch my breath. But, God, in His infinite wisdom, has already prepared our life-preserving armor (see Ephesians 6:10-18), we just need to remember to put it on, each and every morning. When I realized the graciousness of God's provision, I was able to use the artillery of Scripture to extinguish the enemy's fire, leaving him smoking in the distance.

To protect yourself and others around you, you must properly and thoroughly dress for battle. Identify those areas of your life where you are gasping for air and where your exhalations pollute those around you. Tonight, as you prepare for bed, ask the Giver of Life to sanitize your polluted spirit with freshness and purity. Breathe in His goodness; you'll rest so much better!

DAY 34
To Bask in His Glory

Breakfast

"But for you who revere My name, the sun of righteousness will rise with healing in its wings." (Malachi 4:2a)

⚜ **Daily Bread** – Read: Ephesians 5:13-14

"Great job!" "Good work." "I'm so proud of you!" My children love that affirmation even more than "Yes, I'll be happy to buy that for you!" How innate it is for children to seek their parents' approval and try to please them. How sad that, so often in this society, we are all told that our best just isn't good enough. "Try harder!" "Do better." "Achieve more!"

The Lord does desire more from His children. He does not want us to settle for "good" when he has the very best in mind for us! The pursuit of God, however, is completely different than our earthly pursuits. We seek God in weakness, not strength. We experience victory, not in how hard we try, but in how much we trust. We get direction from the Scriptures, preparation while we wait, and resources only when we begin. The Bible tells us that the first will be last and the last will be first (Mark 10:31), the meek will inherit the earth (Matthew 5:5), and those who are faithful will receive the crown of Life (Revelation 2:10).

The prophet, Habakkuk, struggled to comprehend God's ways, confused in his perception of good and evil, just and unjust. Eventually, he learned to wait patiently in faith and to trust in the all-knowing wisdom of God. In Habakkuk 3:4, the prophet provides a glorious description of God: *"His splendor was like the sunrise; rays flashed from His hand, where His power was hidden."*

The approval of our Heavenly Father rests squarely on our faithfulness. We please Him with our belief and trust. In what ways are you trusting Him this morning?

_____
_____
_____
_____
_____

Lunch

"The LORD will keep you from all harm – He will watch over your life; the LORD will watch over your coming and going both now and forevermore."
(Psalm 121:7-8)

⚜ **Daily Bread** – Read: Numbers 6:24-26

Meditate on your Daily Bread for just a moment. The Old Testament mentions the back of God many times, but God did not show His face to even His most faithful followers because the very sight of His glory would have killed them on the spot. Even Moses had to veil his own face when He returned to the Israelites after living in the presence of God on Mt. Sinai because the glow of his own face intensely radiated the splendor of the Lord.

What a tremendous blessing to have God's face shine upon you! When He gazes at us, He sees us as we really are. His vision goes beyond our poorly applied layers and crudely built walls. He looks at our heart (1 Samuel 16:7), and He knows our every need. When Hagar met the Lord in the desert, she said, *"You are the God who sees me."* (Genesis 16:13).

The Lord loves to meet us in our time of need, and He delights in making Himself known. While we might not always notice His presence, He always is watching over us.

Thank Him for always watching over you, and pray Numbers 6:24-26 as a blessing on behalf of someone who could use a glimpse of God right now.

_____
_____
_____
_____
_____
_____

Dinner

"But whoever lives by the truth comes into the light, so that it may be seen plainly that what he has done has been done through God."
(John 3:21)

⚜ **Daily Bread** – Read: Isaiah 60:1-3

I recently had an amazing time of rest with the Lord. My husband blessed me with a three-day retreat at a local hotel, so I could pray and be alone with God. The Lord distinctly called me to come away, and I now refer to that time as my three days in the whale's belly.

I really looked forward to my sanctuary with the Lord; my desire was not about running from Him (as Jonah did) but running to Him, falling into His arms, and confessing my sins and weaknesses.

I had read Bill Bright's book, *The Coming Revival,* and, in one chapter which detailed how to prepare for a fast, he listed a series of questions regarding sins in your life. (See appendix for recommending reading.) In my seclusion, I answered each item on the list, writing down my sins and praying over them with the recommended Scriptures.

My prayer of confession lasted for over an hour, and what happened during that time was nothing short of glorious. My eyes were closed, my cheeks were soaked with tears from crying and from pouring my heart out to God, and, as I prayed, the brilliance of the afternoon sun poured through the window sheers and engulfed the entire room. I had been shivering from the coldness of the air conditioned room, and, all of a sudden, I was cloaked in warmth and light. I felt extreme calm and peace, as well as the realization that I wasn't alone. I tried to open my eyes to catch a glimpse of the awesome presence I was sensing, but the light was much too bright. I felt what I couldn't see, and it was undoubtedly the pleasure of my Heavenly Father, delighted that I had been obedient and come to the place where He wanted to meet me. It wasn't about going to a secluded hotel room, because the location wasn't important. It was about the spiritual place, the point of repentance and forgiveness.

What I've found is that you can't be fully surrendered to Christ – you can't be fully His – until you give Him all of yourself, and all includes every last bit of the ugliness, the sin, the struggle, and the pain that you may have been hiding. God wants to free us from the burdens that have shackled us, so we are unfettered to do the work that He is calling us to do.

He's calling all of us – you, too! Most of us, though, are held hostage by the world to such an extent that we are of little use for His Kingdom. What a shame and a waste! He desires so much more for His children! He longs for each of us to bask in His glow, to feel the warmth and comfort of His presence and the joy and satisfaction of His pleasure.

On that day in the hotel room, the Lord confirmed to me that there are many things we can do to bring Him pleasure, but none equal a humble and earnest prayer of confession and repentance. Tonight, as the darkness settles, take a moment to settle yourself into the brilliance of your Father's Light, and compose your own personal prayer of confession to the Lord.

_____
_____
_____
_____
_____
_____
_____
_____
_____
_____
_____
_____
_____
_____
_____
_____
_____

DAY 35
A Matter of the Heart

Breakfast

*"For the word of God is living and active. Sharper than any double-edged sword, it
penetrates even to dividing soul and spirit, joints and marrow;
it judges the thoughts and attitudes of the heart."*
(Hebrews 4:12)

✣ Daily Bread – Read: 1 Samuel 16:7

You only get one chance to make a first impression. We've all heard that adage. Unfortunately, in today's society, the better the outside wrapping, the better the impression. In the judgment of the viewing public, if the exterior is acceptable, it doesn't matter what secrets and troubles are untidily tucked inside.

When David was a boy, his older brothers were built like warriors, but David, the youngest, had the heart of a warrior, and he was God's chosen one to defeat Goliath, the nine-foot tall, ferocious, and so far undefeated, champion. To the unenlightened public, those odds didn't look so good for David, but in the Lord's economy, Goliath's days were numbered.

We can dress it up, paint it on, or squeeze it in, but God sees through the plastic façade that fools others. After all, the unseen, and often unsightly, parts of us are what He most desires. Our outer covering, our physical human body, is a temporary shell that will eventually be set aside and made new, glorified.

The Lord's concern is for your innermost being, which He diligently and thoughtfully planned before you were in your mother's womb (Jeremiah 1:5). Inside us, too, is where His real image and likeness dwells (Genesis 1:26) including His righteousness and holiness (Ephesians 4:24), and His knowledge (Colossians 3:10).

God constantly searches and examines our hearts for hidden character and motive. The character He desires to surface is His own reflection, and the motive He wishes to uncover is love.

What is the condition of your heart? When God looks upon you and searches deep within you, what does He find?

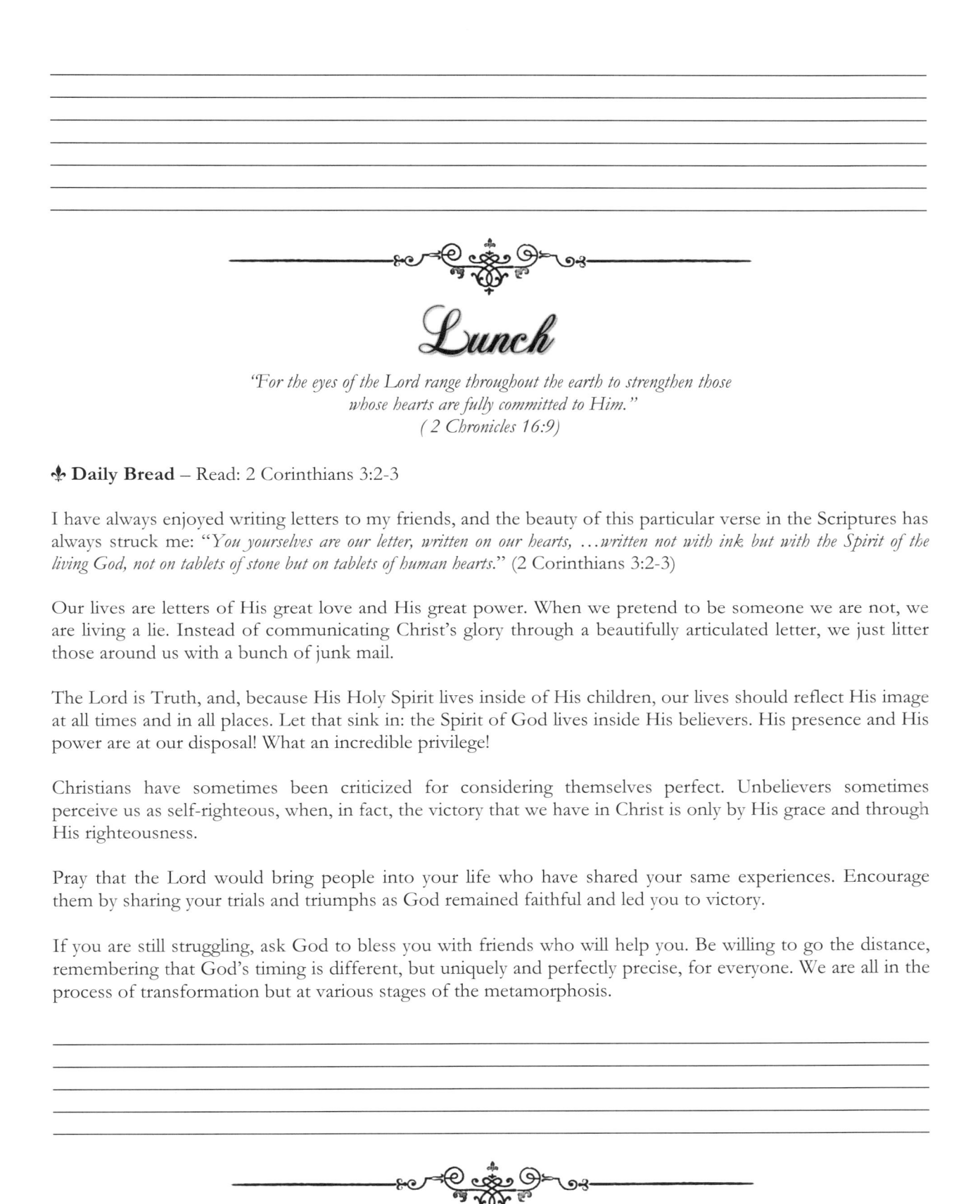

Lunch

"For the eyes of the Lord range throughout the earth to strengthen those whose hearts are fully committed to Him."
(2 Chronicles 16:9)

⚜ **Daily Bread** – Read: 2 Corinthians 3:2-3

I have always enjoyed writing letters to my friends, and the beauty of this particular verse in the Scriptures has always struck me: *"You yourselves are our letter, written on our hearts, …written not with ink but with the Spirit of the living God, not on tablets of stone but on tablets of human hearts."* (2 Corinthians 3:2-3)

Our lives are letters of His great love and His great power. When we pretend to be someone we are not, we are living a lie. Instead of communicating Christ's glory through a beautifully articulated letter, we just litter those around us with a bunch of junk mail.

The Lord is Truth, and, because His Holy Spirit lives inside of His children, our lives should reflect His image at all times and in all places. Let that sink in: the Spirit of God lives inside His believers. His presence and His power are at our disposal! What an incredible privilege!

Christians have sometimes been criticized for considering themselves perfect. Unbelievers sometimes perceive us as self-righteous, when, in fact, the victory that we have in Christ is only by His grace and through His righteousness.

Pray that the Lord would bring people into your life who have shared your same experiences. Encourage them by sharing your trials and triumphs as God remained faithful and led you to victory.

If you are still struggling, ask God to bless you with friends who will help you. Be willing to go the distance, remembering that God's timing is different, but uniquely and perfectly precise, for everyone. We are all in the process of transformation but at various stages of the metamorphosis.

Dinner

" 'Even now' declares the LORD, 'return to Me with all your heart, with fasting and weeping and mourning.' Rend your heart and not your garments."
(Joel 2:12-13a)

⚜ **Daily Bread** – Read: Hebrews 10:19-25

The entire landscape of the church is changing, along with the traditional structure of the local church, as seekers of Christ look for Him in unconventional places. Jesus is who He says He is, and He came to meet us right where we are – on our turf, so to speak. Therefore, today, He encounters us in locations like coffee houses, movie theaters, and college campuses.

Today's seeker isn't necessarily drawn to look for the Jesus of the Bible in long-established, brick-and-mortar sanctuaries. Many believers, longing for unconditional love and acceptance, are becoming disenchanted with the bureaucracy of churches. Tragically, more and more people are walking out of the church doors, never to return. I have met several couples recently who used to be great servants in the church just a few short years ago but who now do not attend church at all. Why?

Jesus was living proof that God can be met anywhere His people are. Churches weren't meant to build walls and close doors. As tonight's Daily Bread Scripture indicates, church was designed for fellowship with other believers. We are designed to celebrate and worship the Lord together, as one body. After renewing ourselves with fellow believers, we're then to take Him out into the world, into our communities, workplaces, and neighborhoods.

Because His Spirit lives inside us, He goes wherever we go. We need to be in fellowship with other believers so we can build each other up and share how His Spirit is working in our lives. What are we learning? How is He transforming us? Who are we reaching? If our desire is to love God and to spend time with Him, then we must also love and spend time with His children, who are made in His image.

Outside a church, I once saw a sign that posed the question, "Are we an audience or an army?" Many postmodern churches have fallen into the trap of entertaining their congregations instead of inspiring them. Churches can fall into the trap of competing with the world to attract the multitudes; instead of having people rise to meet the standards of Almighty God, the bar is lowered to reach the lowest common denominator.

God is the same yesterday, today, and tomorrow. Hebrews 13:8 confirms, *"Jesus Christ is the same yesterday and today and forever."* People will eventually tire of entertaining presentations, but they will never grow weary of the True and Living God. Our God is so full of mystery, awe, wonder, and wisdom that there is no need to accessorize Him with irrelevant and superfluous fluff.

When we come to church, we expect that the Lord is at work. We easily see Him on Sunday morning, but we need help identifying Him the other six days of the week. Paul encourages in Galatians 6:9-10, *"Let us not become weary in doing good, for at the proper time we will reap a harvest if we do not give up. Therefore, as we have opportunity, let us do good to all people, especially to those who belong to the family of believers."*

"Don't grow weary *watching* others do good" is not the exhortation. We must be active participants in our church and in our communities, continually serving as the hands and feet of Jesus. *"You are the light of the world,"* Jesus proclaimed to His believers. *"…let your light shine before men, that they may see your good deeds and praise your Father in heaven."* (See Matthew 5:14-16).

Does the heartbeat of your church match the rhythm of God's? Pray for your church leaders, and pray for opportunities to serve in your church. Pray that all who come through its doors will experience the complete love of God.

A Worthy Vessel

*"They devoted themselves to the apostles' teaching and to the fellowship,
to the breaking of bread and to prayer."*
(Acts 2:42)

Your usefulness to God stems not from the type of vessel you were but from the type of vessel you've become.

When you first entered the world, your vessel, was blemished with the stain of sin, as all of us are. As the years progressed, your vessel became chipped and cracked, worn and faded, unstable and useless. When you finally realized your human limitations and weaknesses, you fell on your knees before God, and poured out your remaining contents at His feet.

You asked Him to accept you as you were, scuffed and scarred, and you beseeched Him to refill you with His love, mercy, and grace. And, of course, the Lord was waiting and willing to do so. He never gave up on you.

Like a shepherd diligently searching for His lost sheep, the Lord prayed that you would, one day, ask to be found. He heard your cries as you were snagged in thorns and briars; He untangled you from the brambles and carried you away in His arms. You were dirty, tattered, tired, and worn, but it didn't matter what you looked like or how He found you. You were safe at last, secure in His loving embrace.

God's plan is not just to rescue you but to cleanse you in His righteousness, clothe you in royal robes, and feed you from the King's table. As the father rejoiced in the return of his prodigal son, your Heavenly Father rejoiced in your return. Yet you will not remain as He found you, for He is transforming you into the person He planned for you to be.

You've strayed. You've run away. You've fallen into the pit. You've been wounded. You were lost, but now you're found, and your Hero accepted you just the way you were. But, His love exceeds bandaged bruises and kissed boo-boos; it requires Him to perform a little open heart surgery.

Your original vessel was covered in dirty dressings, soiled shreds, and pitiful patches. You were hanging by a thread, unstable and becoming unglued. Your feeble attempts to keep yourself together under your own power were rapidly unraveling.

You are still a work in progress, but, oh, what He sees beyond your tattered and torn surface is glorious, wonderful, and so incredibly beautiful! He will remove your rust, displace your dust, and burnish you until you are shiny and new.

He is the potter; you are the clay. (Isaiah 64:8). As the wheel of life spins and you feel out of control, remember Who has His hands firmly around you. You are safe in His care. Keep your eyes on Him, and remember that He is in control.

Sometimes the pressure seems unbearable as His Hands press in on you, but the greater the pressure, the more He is shaping and molding you. He will never release His grip. That is the wonder of His love; He is always there, and the more painful life becomes, the tighter He holds you.

Malachi 3:3a says, *"He will sit as a refiner and purifier of silver."* Do you know how a silversmith refines silver? He holds it over the fire and heats it right in the middle of the fire, where the flames are the hottest, to burn away all of the impurities. He can't just leave the silver there alone; he must keep his eyes on it at all times. Left for just a moment too long, it can be completely destroyed. And, as the silver is painstakingly and thoroughly refined, do you know how the silversmith knows when it is pure enough? It is ready when he sees his image reflected in it.

If you're feeling the heat of the fire, remember that God's eye is on you. He is holding you and watching you until He sees His image in you.

Your 40-day journey with the Lord has taken you to the greatest heights and the lowest depths. You chose to experience physical pain, emotional pain, and mental pain because you were willing to believe Him and take Him at His Word. You've squeezed a lifetime of pain, difficulty, perseverance, and reward into a relatively minute amount of time – not for the pride of saying that you accomplished a great feat but for the privilege of accomplishing His great Will. Knowing that He's reliably carried you through this experience, imagine what lies ahead because of your obedience and faithfulness!

God uses willing hearts. Your willingness to go where He leads you, regardless of the cost, the uncertainty, or the lack of human resources, delights Him. His prayer for you is that you will love as He has loved. Your cracked and common vessel, once crudely glued together, has been shattered. Your loving Father took those tiny shards, one by one, into His precious hands, and He refashioned them into a glorious and worthy vessel held together with the unbreakable bond of His awesome love. He restored you, filled you, sharpened your vision, and clarified your purpose.

Your life is no longer a dull and worthless clay pot but a sparkling and invaluable crystal receptacle, luminous with the Light of Jesus Christ. When He gazes at you now, He sees His reflection radiated like a million stars in the heavens, and He celebrates the new life He is creating in you.

You are a worthy vessel ready to be emptied yet again, this time as an offering and testimony of His love and grace. And, He has called you to fast again; however, you will not dine alone with Him. His Divine plan now calls you to set the table for the multitudes. Isaiah 58:6-12 is His example and your mandate. Read it, remember it, and resolve to live it.

DAY 36

Available

Breakfast

"God can use us only in the place where He calls us."
— Corrie ten Boom

⚜ **Daily Bread** – Read: Matthew 28:18-20

One Sunday afternoon, as I watched the televised sermon of Dr. Charles Stanley, senior pastor of First Baptist Church Atlanta, he said something that really stuck with me. "Make yourself available to God," he urged, "and watch Him work."

I have seen God work in so many wonderful and miraculous ways over the years, and my most sincere prayer has been that everything I do and say will bring honor and glory to Jesus' name. However, He can only use what is made available to Him.

At the beginning of the fast, you learned about distraction – one of Satan's greatest tactics to hinder God's children from His service. The enemy knows that if we are consumed with too many tasks – even worthy ministerial opportunities – we will be too busy to spend time with God, too busy to pray, too busy to study God's Word, and too busy to hear His direction.

Billy Graham said of Corrie ten Boom, "She is a living example of how the Lord works in the life of a person who is surrendered to His leading and His will."

Corrie admitted that she lost her first Love for a while but found Him again in a German concentration camp. After surviving ten months of incarceration, a paperwork fluke technically freed her, but she knew that God's grace released her. She lost her father and beloved sister to the horrors of the Nazi death camp, but after her improbable release, she confessed, "(I had) a love for the people around me – a burning desire to tell them that Jesus is a reality, that He lives, that He is victor…I wanted everyone to know that no matter how deep we fall, the Everlasting Arms are always under us to carry us out." That is what happens when Jesus saves us.

Only through an unimaginably horrendous trial did her testimony become strong. The life she lived was real; the atrocity she endured was true. Truer still were the loving arms of God that carried her through each moment of her pain and suffering. Corrie lived the remainder of her life being available for Jesus.

There are many saints like her living today. To me, Dr. Stanley personifies obedience and faithfulness to the Lord. Without the commitment and availability of these willing servants, and others like them, to acknowledge God's call, many of us would be robbed from experiencing God's great love and power through them.

Do you realize that God is calling you, too? When you fast unto the Lord, you are in a period of preparation. You must be willing and obedient to follow the Spirit's lead. Absorb God's teaching and training, and then, act upon it. Ask the Lord to lead you to the field that is ripe for harvest (John 4:35), and be willing to go where He directs.

Lunch

"First we listened to God's plan; then we signed it. This was unlike the method
I once used when I made my own plans and then asked God to sign them.
Our desire was to be 'planned' by the Holy Spirit."
— Corrie ten Boom, Tramp for the Lord

⚜ **Daily Bread** – Read: Acts 1:4-5, 8

From the moment you accept Jesus as Lord and Savior of your life, He prepares you to spread the Good News. It is a plan He designed well before the creation of the world. This plan is evidenced by the gift of His Holy Spirit which indwells every believer. Through His Spirit, you receive His power.

The Lord calls all of us to represent His love and grace to our families, our neighbors, and our co-workers. He calls us to bear witness in our communities, across our nation, and in the far corners of the earth.

Most of us are not gifted with the evangelism of Billy Graham, but we all have received the same Spirit, and we all are gifted to share the gospel message. Each of us has been placed right where the Lord wants us, and He has gifted us accordingly. He has specifically equipped each of us for a particular function whether it is teaching, serving, caring, or anything else. (Romans 12:6-8)

If you are not aware of your unique spiritual gifts, pray for the Lord to fully reveal them to you. When He does, use them for His glory! If you know or are just beginning discover your spiritual gifts, write them down. Seek the Lord's Will for the best use of your gifts. Pray for His guidance as you sift the service opportunities that come your way.

Dinner

"Because of my chains, most of the brothers in the Lord have been encouraged to speak the Word of God more courageously and fearlessly."
(Philippians 1:14)

⚜ **Daily Bread** – Read: 2 Timothy 1:6-7

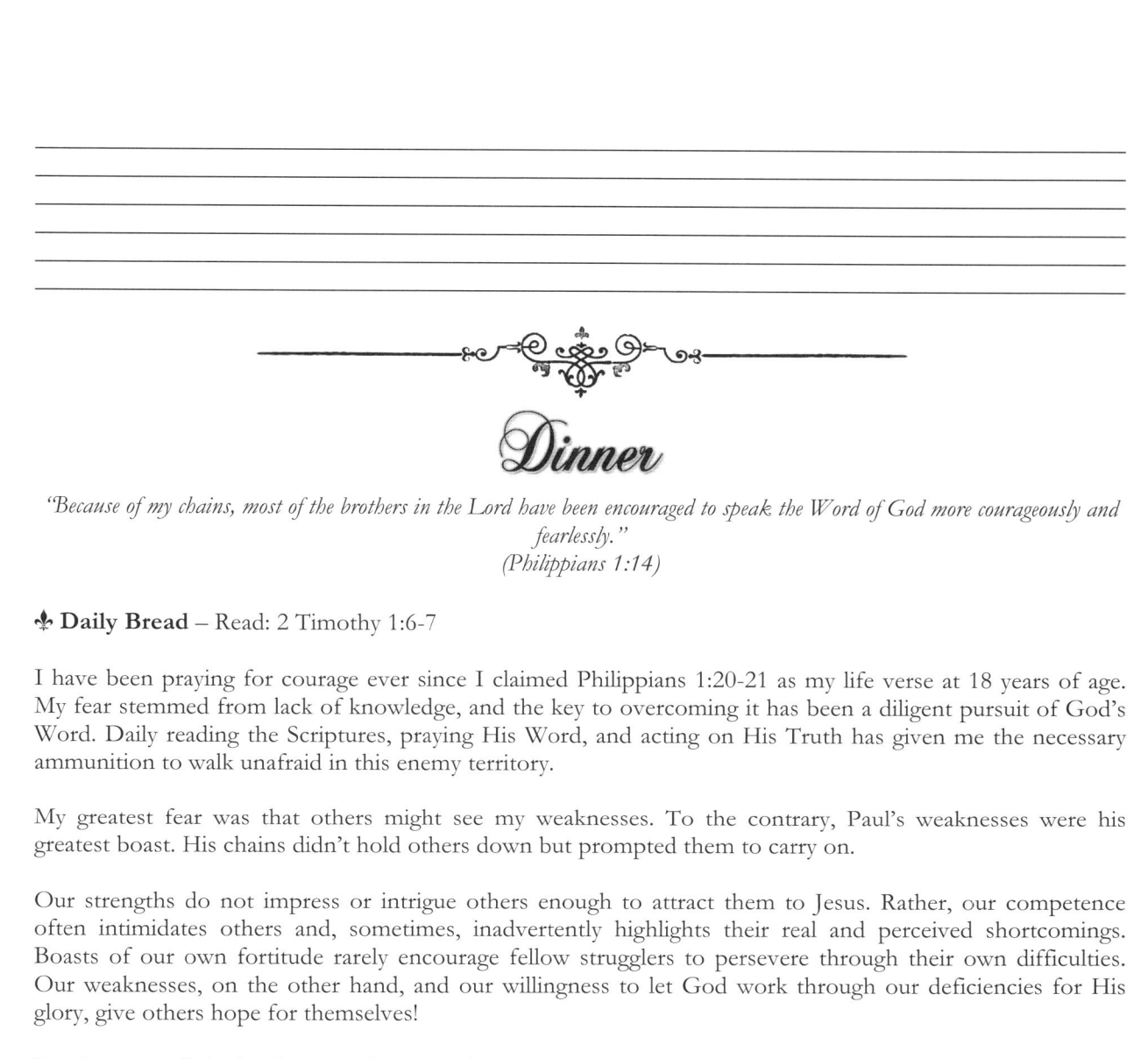

I have been praying for courage ever since I claimed Philippians 1:20-21 as my life verse at 18 years of age. My fear stemmed from lack of knowledge, and the key to overcoming it has been a diligent pursuit of God's Word. Daily reading the Scriptures, praying His Word, and acting on His Truth has given me the necessary ammunition to walk unafraid in this enemy territory.

My greatest fear was that others might see my weaknesses. To the contrary, Paul's weaknesses were his greatest boast. His chains didn't hold others down but prompted them to carry on.

Our strengths do not impress or intrigue others enough to attract them to Jesus. Rather, our competence often intimidates others and, sometimes, inadvertently highlights their real and perceived shortcomings. Boasts of our own fortitude rarely encourage fellow strugglers to persevere through their own difficulties. Our weaknesses, on the other hand, and our willingness to let God work through our deficiencies for His glory, give others hope for themselves!

I no longer walk in fear because I've tapped into the power of the Holy Spirit. I've accepted, even embraced, my weaknesses, and I've realize that they have actually been a blessing to me. My fears caused me to dig deeper into God's Word and to rely on Him instead of myself. That is His plan! He does not want us to be deceived by the world's push for self-sufficiency. We must realize that our sufficiency comes only from Him. His grace is enough! (See 2 Corinthians 12:9).

Tonight, as you pray, cast your fears at God's feet. Ask Him to reveal how you can more fully rely on the power of His indwelling Holy Spirit. Search the Scriptures for examples of your particular weaknesses, and find encouragement from others who made themselves available to God despite their imperfections and found great victory in Christ Jesus.

DAY 37

Center

Breakfast

"So whether you eat or drink or whatever you do, do it for the glory of God."
(1 Corinthians 10:31)

⚜ **Daily Bread** – Read: Psalm 104:1-5

The Lord desires to be the center of our lives – our very heart and souls. The evidence of Jesus should exist there. His commands should be written on our hearts. His Holy Word should be engraved in our minds. His character should be fully reflected in our behaviors.

You are nearing the end of your fast, whether you persevered 40 days in a row, one day a week, or anything in between. God is so proud of your faithfulness and desire to seek Him! Unadulterated love for the Lord, not legalism, enhances your relationship with Him; you know Him more deeply and intimately, and you've experienced first-hand His compassion as your Father, Savior, and Friend.

At this point, your desire is no longer for food. The cravings you once felt for things of this world have been stifled. The grumbling in your stomach has turned into a hunger for something more. Your weakened state has been replaced by a fervor to get up and go! You have been restored with new energy and new focus. You eyes are fixed solely on Jesus.

Your selfish desires are diminished, and your worldly cravings are dulled. Your meaningless grumblings, which kept you perpetually off-center and out of balance, have righted themselves through your gratitude for God's great grace.

Today, express your appreciation to the Lord for stabilizing you in His love and mercy. Praise Him for the gift of His personal relationship. You've returned to your first Love!

_____
_____
_____
_____
_____
_____
_____

Lunch

"We take captive every thought to make it obedient to Christ."
(2 Corinthians 10:5b)

⚜ **Daily Bread** – Read: Proverbs 4:20-27

Jesus is not a moving target. He is right in front of you all the time. He has gone before you, and prepared the way. In fact, He knows exactly where you're heading right now, and He's already prepared the emergency route to redirect your missed exits and wrong turns. Just keep your eyes on Him, and your path will be straight.

"Enter through the narrow gate," the Lord teaches in Matthew 7:13. *"For wide is the gate and broad is the road that leads to destruction, and many enter through it. But small is the gate and narrow the road that leads to life, and only a few find it."*

Jesus is the bull's eye at the center of the target. He is the light at the end of the tunnel. If you take your eyes off of Him for even a moment, you will miss the mark and fumble in darkness. You can not miss a single Divine meal, or the world will disorient you faster than you can turn around.

It is mind-bending to realize that God's magnificent love is focused on a tiny ball of blue and green floating in His vast universe. Even more profound is that the Lord's most precious creation exists on that relatively small sphere.

My friend, do not drift off track at this stage of your journey; you're on the home stretch now! Maintain your equilibrium by remaining in Him. Maximize your ability to go the distance by consciously choosing to reorient yourself at His Divine rest stops. Bypassing Him will not get you to your destination quicker; you will only find yourself stranded and off-course.

This afternoon, center yourself in God's great love for you. Reflect upon the stunning consideration that He created you for such a time as this (read the story of Esther, particularly 4:14). You have an anointed purpose; do not stray to the right or the left, or you may miss what God has placed before you.

Dinner

"I have been crucified with Christ and I no longer live, but Christ lives in me."
(Galatians 2:20a)

⚜ **Daily Bread** – Read: Psalm 27:4

I recently heard a beautiful song entitled "Center" by Charlie Hall. It is a beautiful prayer for the Lord, who holds all things together, to become the center of our lives. When He truly is the center, all else can be falling apart around us, and it is He who holds us firm.

The closer Christ comes to the center of your life, the more your focus shifts from earthly concerns to a heavenly perspective. Your life rests squarely in His hands; His sufficiency perfectly balances you. Your fleshly impulses have been crucified and replaced with the living glory of God.

This journey, these past 38 days, has been all about that – sitting daily at His table and growing in your desire to be with Him; that no circumstance, difficulty, even blessings or rewards, are enough to pull your attention from the beauty of His holiness.

David, a man after God's own heart, declared the heart of God for His children when he proclaimed, *"One thing I ask of the Lord, this is what I seek: That I may dwell in the house of the Lord all the days of my life, to gaze upon the beauty of the Lord and to seek Him in His temple"* (Psalm 27:4).

Can we say that He has accomplished this in our lives? The Lord is the one pursuing us and He longs for our response to dwell with Him in His temple that we may become a holy temple for Him to dwell with us. The more we sit with Him and learn from Him and fill our minds with thoughts of Him, the less cluttered our lives become and the way is cleared for Him to fill every corner of our lives with Him.

O how our Lord loves to spend this time with us. Pray tonight that He will remain the absolute center of your life. Let everything you do radiate and cascade from that core; let it engulf everyone you meet, so that they may become jealous to know the One in Whom your life is fixed.

DAY 38

Consumed

Breakfast

*"I will put my law in their minds and write it on their hearts.
I will be their God and they will be My people."*
(Jeremiah 31:33b)

⚜ **Daily Bread** – Read: Jeremiah 24:7

God created our hearts to know Him. He relentlessly pursues us through our wrong turns and missed opportunities, and patiently reroutes us towards His intended destination. Like the faithful shepherd consumed with finding his one lost and wandering sheep, the Lord does not give up on us until we are safely back in His fold.

Once we've rested in His safe and loving arms, it's hard to understand why any of His children would ever be compelled to wander. The thought that one would stray from Him seems alien and ridiculous, but we do not yet dwell in the perfection of our eternal home, and, well, evil happens. Sometimes, our trials and difficulties seem all-consuming, and the battles exhaust us. But, have you read the back of the Book? We're not losers. God wins. We are victors!

Once captivated by the love and forgiveness of our Savior, we can become held hostage by the demands of daily life. Sometimes, God's children forget Him, but He never, ever forgets us. He is forever watching us, calling us back to Him, beckoning us to return to the place we once knew.

Are you resting safely in your Savior's arms? Does the familiarity of His warm embrace hug you like a favorite blanket? Do you know that He is always watching you, even when you wander?

Moses wandered in the desert and became so captivated by the burning bush and the presence of the Lord that his heart was set on fire to do the things of God. Have you begun to feel the flicker of that original flame, God set in your heart, start to burn with more intensity these past few weeks with the Lord? The Lord desires for you to return to Him with all your heart. May your heart always be on fire for Him.

As your day begins, consider the condition of your heart. Have you seen a difference in your priorities since you've been consumed with the Lord these six weeks? Praise God for His attentiveness and willingness to relentlessly pursue you.

_____
_____
_____
_____
_____
_____
_____
_____
_____
_____

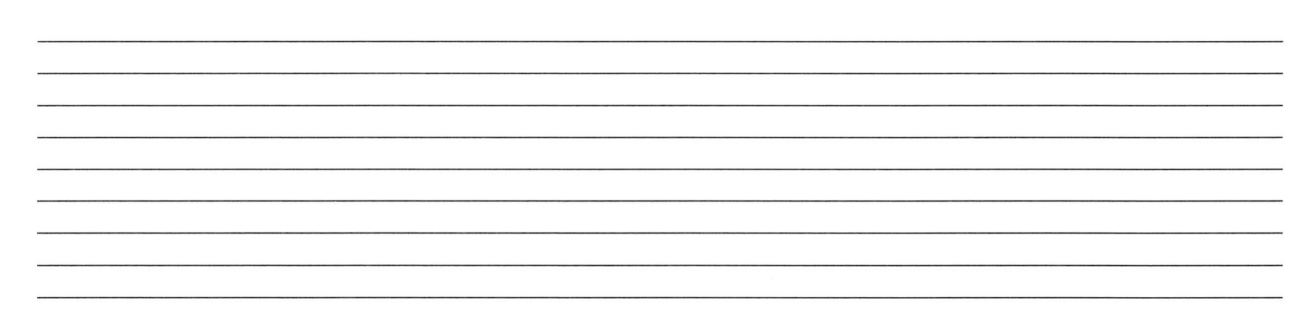

Lunch

"For the LORD your God is a consuming fire..."
(Deuteronomy 4:24)

⚜ **Daily Bread** – Read: Daniel 3:8-18

Fire is amazing. It is a brilliant array of color, and it provides incredible warmth. Yet, it is also very dangerous. The center burns the hottest, and the closer you get to the flame, the greater your risk of injury. However, fire will eventually die down and grow cold unless more fuel is added.

So it is with the will of God. It's been said the being in the center of God's will is the most dangerous place to be. The more obedient we are, the more consumed we are with following God's plan for our lives, and the greater risk we are willing to take.

At the very center of His will is His awesome power, which is also available to us when we surrender our selfish pursuits to His Divine purposes. When you enter the presence of God, the walls you've erected around yourself eventually combust under the white-heat intensity of your earnest desire to surrender to the Living Lord. Before you know it, your carefully built walls are a pile of harmless ash, and His presence is free to spread like wildfire.

Being on fire for the Lord is a powerful and overwhelming emotion. The story of Shadrach, Meshach, and Abednego is a dynamic example of believers willing to be literally set on fire on behalf of the Lord. As they faced King Nebuchadnezzar's blazing furnace, which had been purposely made seven times hotter than usual and emitted heat extreme enough to kill the king's soldiers who stood outside it, these men signified that they were consumed not by demands or pressures of the world but solely by God's will. As it turns out, if you've read the story, they were not consumed by the fiery furnace, either, all praise to God!

Few of us will ever have to make a stand for God before a flaming furnace, but, every day, there are millions who face a similar eternal fate. As we know from Matthew 28:19-20, the Great Commission Jesus gave His followers was to *"go and make disciples of all nations"*. Every day that we choose our own priorities over this command, we are out of God's Will.

Consider the things that are displacing God's call in your life. Don't be overwhelmed and consumed by your daily checklist; if you put His priority above your own, you'll be tackling the most important thing first, and the rest won't seem so important or urgent.

Don't become distracted by fighting fires that God did not call you to extinguish, but pray for Him to douse the unsanctified flames that try to devour you. Then, add fuel to His Holy and all-consuming fire by remaining in His Word and in communication with Him.

_____
_____
_____
_____
_____
_____
_____
_____
_____
_____

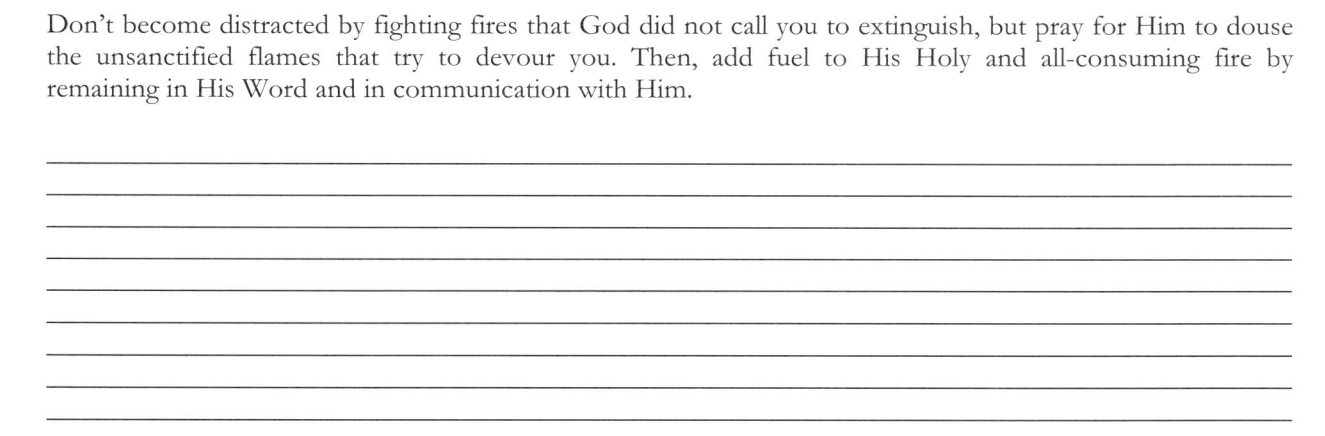

Dinner

*"Because of the LORD's great love we are not consumed, for His compassions never fail.
They are new every morning; great is Your faithfulness. I say to myself,
"The LORD is my portion; therefore I will wait for Him."*
(Lamentations 3:22-24)

⚜ **Daily Bread** – Read: Philippians 3:7-11

When we become consumed with God, everything thing else tends to fade away. Our gain is God; our loss is, well, our loss really doesn't matter. The apostle Paul counted everything as loss except for the privilege of knowing God. If we can truly embrace Paul's example, we can let go of the worldly things that are shackling us to fleshly and selfish pursuits.

God's desire is that we know Him; yet, somehow, we've decided that accepting His Son as Savior is good enough. We've checked the box without reading the fine print. There are 66 books of specifications which spell out the many details of God's character, if we'll just take the time to read and study them. In any contract, when we fail to read the fine print, and when things begin to fall apart, we wonder how it could have happened. If we read the document, we'll be familiar with the terms.

When you read the Bible, you'll see that, no matter what you're experiencing, someone else has already been there and done that. You also learn that even the most righteous of believers were all still human and therefore made mistakes, but God loved them anyway.

Entering into a trust agreement with a gentlemen's handshake is a great thing. But, when we accepted God's covenant, we agreed to more that just believing in Him. Knowing God takes commitment. To truly know Him means to be consumed by Him. To be consumed by Him means that He permeates every fiber of your being. And, that level of familiarity takes complete dedication and unswerving devotion.

Our covenant with God is not something to stick in a drawer and pull out only when something goes wrong. We are not supposed to refer to it every now and then. We need to be thoroughly knowledgeable and completely educated about its contents.

We can spend our entire Christian lives standing by, just watching God work, or we can step out in faith, dive into the center of His will, and become consumed by Him. We can be idle bystanders in the work of Christ or vital and active participants in furthering His Kingdom.

Which are you: an amazed observer or an active participant? I heard a quote once that went something like this, "*We can't all be heroes. Someone has to stand on the sidewalk and clap as the parade goes by.*" Let me clarify right now that God doesn't want you standing on the sidewalk! You're supposed to be in the procession!

Participation requires that you actively seek Him, and that is a daily pursuit. Take some time tonight to familiarize yourself with His fine print. Then, record the steps you will take to step off of the sidewalk and into the parade.

DAY 39

Masterpiece

Breakfast

"And we, who with unveiled faces all reflect the Lord's glory, are being transformed into His likeness with ever-increasing glory, which comes from the Lord, who is the Spirit." –
(2 Corinthians 3:18)

⚜ Daily Bread – Read: Micah 6:8

My children love to draw; I have piles and piles of their little masterpieces stuffed into many boxes. Every so often, these little works of art seem to grow feet and find their way to my table tops and my bedroom floor.

At the end of my bed is a blanket chest, filled to the brim with these precious art projects created by my three children. One day, my youngest daughter decided to unearth this treasure chest, and she told me she wanted to redecorate my room. As I was studying on my bed, I watched her as she diligently made her mess – I mean her masterpiece.

Soon she exclaimed, "Look how beautiful your room is!" Amazingly, in such a short time span, she managed to cover my entire armoire as well as every photo frame, door knob, and drawer within her reach. My room looked like a kindergarten art museum. She was so happy that these treasures were no longer hidden in the dark.

I once did try to dispose of an older stack of my children's artwork, but my son found it in the trash and was very upset that I was throwing away such important papers. I have since resigned myself to keeping them and have worked to overcome my obsessive need to get rid of "clutter" and "junk". I decided it was more important to allow my children to grow up knowing that every little part of their lives is a cherished and important part of mine, no matter how sticky, tacky, and glittery some of those parts may be.

Only through the eyes of a parent can we see the beauty in our children's messes. It is the same with our Heavenly Father when He looks upon all the messes we make in our lives. He sees the beauty while we see the ashes. He sees the potential while we see the problems. He sees a work completed while we see a work in progress. We live in the batter of the mixing bowl, but He sees the beautifully finished cake.

Our Heavenly Father knows what the finished product will look like. He knows what we are capable of if we just rest in His capable hands. He makes masterpieces from our messes! Just like any good parent who cleans up after the mess is made, the Lord is always there to pick up even the tiniest scraps we leave in the wake of our untidy lives. He is always working to restore His own created treasures – you, me, and all of His children – plucking us out of the trash, freeing us from the dark, and proudly displaying us for the world to see.

Have you gained a greater clarity into what the Lord wants to do in your life? Are you beginning to understand the process? Do you have a clearer picture of His plans and purposes for you? Take time to record the journey you have taken in your life so far, and highlight the snapshots of the Lord's faithfulness. Look, too, for the broad strokes He's granted you in His willingness to let you make mistakes and messes along the way.

Praise Him that no matter how big of a mess you make, He is always there to help you clean up, pick up the pieces, and start anew. Express your gratitude that He does not become overwhelmed by your mounting clutter and throw you out but that He patiently and lovingly continues His process of shaping you into the treasured masterpiece He created you to be.

___

Lunch

"Instead, it should be that of your inner self, the unfading beauty of a gentle and quiet spirit, which is of great worth in God's sight."
(1 Peter 3:3-4)

⚜ **Daily Bread** – Read: Ephesians 2:10

As a teenager, I had the privilege of attending the Basic Youth Conflicts conference taught by Bill Gothard in Eugene, Oregon. I really loved these conferences, and often, my mom and I attended together.

As Mr. Gothard spoke, he began painting a beautiful picture, not only in words but with an artist brush. It was extraordinary to hear the Scriptures as I watched a masterpiece in progress. It wasn't until he finished speaking that the audience could see what the picture was meant to be.

When we read the Bible in its entirety, we see a perfect picture of God's plan for mankind – His promises to His people, His protection of those He loves, and His constant provision of those He calls His own. In everything, from the detail of a bounteous meal created out of next to nothing to the bold focal point of His Son's great sacrifice, God created an incredible presentation in just 66 books, spanning from the beginning of time to the approaching end of the ages.

It's easy to get caught up in all the countless brush strokes of life and the jumbled mix of colors; sometimes, we lose sight of the big picture, and we can't see the proverbial forest for the trees. But, God has a plan for every stroke, every color, and every pattern. He doesn't erase them or toss out the mottled canvas and begin again. He is the ever-patient artist, carefully creating, thoughtfully planning, and lovingly examining every area of our life. He doesn't grow weary of recreating us but uses the many layers which comprise our individual portraits to give us depth and dimension.

On close examination, the hundreds of tiny brush strokes in an impressionist painting like the work of Monet, Manet, or Renoir, don't seem to make any sense. Only at a distance does the jumbled mess of color morph into an awe-inspiring masterpiece.

In his book, *Storm Warning*, the great evangelist Billy Graham told a story of visiting the Louvre Museum in Paris. As he stood at arm's length from a large impressionistic painting by Renoir, globs of paint seemed splattered incoherently across the canvas. He wasn't impressed and wondered aloud, "What in the world is that?"

His wife, Ruth, said, "Stand back, Bill, and you will see it." Because he was standing too close to the masterpiece, each individual detail overwhelmed him and drowned out the overall effect of the work. But, when he stepped back across the hall, the mystery suddenly disappeared, revealing the beautiful image that the artist intended.

Sometimes, we get bogged down in the details of our own lives. It feels as if we are standing in the middle of a painter's color palette, getting mixed up and swirled into a hundred different color combinations. To the Master Artist, however, we are perfectly shaded and toned; He mixes us until we're just right. His brilliance, evidenced through the stories of our lives, will be shared with generations to come as they stand back and admire God's handiwork.

Your life may seem as jumbled as a preschooler's crayon box, or you may be someone who attempts to line up the crayons neatly in the box, alphabetized by name or sorted by color. Either way, you do not hold your life in your own hands. God created you for the intent and purpose of accomplishing His great work through you. Whether you can see it or not, you are a work of art, and you're on exhibit for all to admire the brilliance and glory of the Lord.

This afternoon, as the details of life threaten to overwhelm you – the endless array of demands, errands, and routines – step back and consider your life with fresh eyes. Notice the enormous attention to detail with which God has colored every aspect of your life, and appreciate that His thoughtful planning only enhances the complete package of your beauty and individuality.

Take care, today, in the places you walk, with the people you see, and with the priorities you set. Be ever aware that you are God's masterpiece, and pray that others may see His unequalled work in your life.

Dinner

"You are worthy, our Lord and God, to receive glory and honor and power, for You created all things, and by Your will they were created and have their being."
(Revelation 4:11)

⚜ **Daily Bread** – Read: Isaiah 61:1-3

Corrie ten Boom often carried an embroidered fabric with her when she traveled and spoke. On one side, the knotted thread and frayed strands were visible – all mixed up, crisscrossed, and twisted together. On the other side, a beautiful gold and silver crown was embroidered, perfectly and flawlessly stitched.

Corrie held up the ugly, messy underside of the fabric and recited this poem:

> "MY LIFE IS BUT A WEAVING BETWEEN MY GOD AND ME.
> I DO NOT CHOOSE THE COLORS, HE WORKETH STEADILY.
> OFT' TIMES HE WEAVETH SORROW, AND I, IN FOOLISH PRIDE
> FORGET HE SEES THE UPPER, AND I, THE UNDERSIDE.
> NOT 'TIL THE LOOM IS SILENT, AND SHUTTLES CEASE TO FLY,
> WILL GOD UNROLL THE CANVAS AND EXPLAIN THE REASON WHY.
> THE DARK THREADS ARE AS NEEDFUL IN THE SKILLFUL WEAVER'S HAND
> AS THE THREADS OF GOLD AND SILVER IN THE PATTERN HE HAS PLANNED."
> -ANONYMOUS

What a beautiful illustration and comparison of how God sees our lives versus how we see our lives. From our limited perspective, we have no idea how the muck and mire in our lives can possibly amount to anything of lasting worth, but God, in His infinite wisdom, uses it all in the beauty and majesty of His great Kingdom plan.

The time you have spent praying and fasting with the Lord has been precious, intimate, and illuminating. I pray that you have gained a greater perspective of the way God is working in your life as well as a better understanding of the fact that He is controlling and creating every stray strand of your life. You may feel all knotted up or at loose ends, but you are a living work of art, personally created by the Living and Almighty God!

Pray for faith and vision to accurately complete every stitch of your life as the Lord instructs you, but don't study the pattern so hard that you fail to see His big picture. Praise Him for creating you to be a part of His wonderful master plan!

DAY 40
The Last Breakfast

Breakfast

" 'Come, follow Me,' Jesus said, 'and I will make you fishers of men.' "
(Matthew 4:19)

✣ **Daily Bread** – Read: Matthew 4:18-20

You began this fast desiring to offer yourself as a living sacrifice, holy and pleasing to God (see Romans 12:1). You ended it becoming a worthy vessel, beneficial and useful in His great and sovereign plan. The Lord has taken you from what you thought was impossible to what you now know as incredible.

In the beginning, you had no way to predict God's purpose for you, but you were certain He was calling you. He wanted more time with you, more trust from you, more obedience from you. And, you honored His invitation.

When Jesus called the disciples to follow him, they couldn't have possibly imagined the journey on which they were trustfully embarking. Yet notice the first two words of the 20th verse in Matthew 4 (italics, my emphasis): "*At once* they left their nets and followed Him."

When Simon Peter and Andrew heard Jesus calling them, they didn't hesitate before dropping their nets and whole-heartedly following Him. In verse 22, James and John also heard Jesus' call and "immediately" followed Him.

Oh, to have that faithful obedience! There were no excuses about having to clean the nets or swab the boat first. These men didn't say, "Well, Lord, I'm kind of in the middle of something here. I've got a busy day, but let me finish up, take care of some things at home, pack my bags, and I'll meet you tomorrow." No, these devoted followers of Christ left instantaneously – no ifs, ands, or buts.

The disciples of Jesus saw Him heal and provide, teach and rebuke, pray and weep. They listened to His parables and heard His authority. They watched in wonder as He walked on water and calmed a stormy sea. They experienced great emotional anguish when He was tested and tortured, nailed to the cross and resurrected from the tomb.

Jesus' short earthly ministry spans all of eternity; He still needs faithful and obedient followers in this generation willing to spread the message of His love and forgiveness. Only those believers who truly understand the depth of His forgiveness and the magnitude of His love will be able to withstand the persecution of the world – a fallen world still trying to destroy the Message as it tried to destroy the Messenger.

Fallen or not, this world holds no power to stand against our risen Savior. The Author of life can not be put to death. Amen!

The message of God's love and sacrifice is simple and true. What in these 40 days has the Lord done in you and through you? He is calling you; do not hang up or put Him on hold. Do not put Him through to voice mail or let someone else beep in on His line. He is calling you today. Answer Him without delay.

___

Lunch

"Rise! Let us go! Here comes My betrayer!"
(Mark 14:42)

✤ **Daily Bread** – Read: Mark 14:32-42

When Simon Peter and the other disciples fell asleep instead of remaining watchful as Jesus had asked, the Lord rebuked them. In their Savior's greatest hour of need, His faithful followers took a nap.

What is so characteristic of us is completely uncharacteristic of God. God is a God of absolutes. There is no "maybe", no "might", no "probably". He *always* watches over us. He *never* leaves nor forsakes us. He *never* falls asleep on us. To the contrary, in the hour of our greatest need, He doesn't leave us stranded - He carries us. We can always and completely rest in Him.

Your time of fasting has taught you many wonderful things that you may have known about your Lord but had not personally experienced. You have learned to follow your Lord, and you've gained insight about how He leads and how you are to follow. His desire now, as you venture out into the world to represent Him, is that you be vigilantly and unceasingly watchful.

Keep your eyes fixed on Him, but be aware of and alert to the impending danger lurking around every corner. The Lord encourages in Isaiah 41:10, "*So do not fear, for I am with you; do not be dismayed, for I am your God. I will strengthen you and help you; I will uphold you with my righteous right hand.*" You should not fear; the Lord is with you. But, you should be prepared.

That is why you must diligently stay in His Word each and every day, throughout the day. You must be equipped with the artillery that will successfully halt the enemy's advances – the memorization of Scripture. In

His Holy Word, the Lord has provided every single thing you need to succeed here on earth until you join Him in your heavenly home.

It's been said, "Divine sovereignty does not negate human responsibility". Just because everything rests in His control, we are not exempt from resting in Him, trusting in Him, and obeying Him. The discipline you have developed over these 40 days is to be the standard for the rest of your life. You can not succeed in overcoming the evil that is to come by resting in the storehouse you have built up. You must persevere, press on, and continually seek Him each and every day from this moment forward. This is no time for napping!

You are walking on enemy territory, and you are a stranger here. You must be appropriately dressed for the land in which you live. Attire yourself in the full armor of Christ. You must be suitably prepared for the purpose to which God calls you. Arm yourself with thorough knowledge of Whom and what you believe. Always be ready with an answer for your faith. Colossians 4:6 instructs, *"Let your conversation be always full of grace, seasoned with salt, so that you may know how to answer everyone."*

Staying in the Lord's Will is not a one-time decision. It requires constancy and consistency; it is a choice that you make every day, moment by moment. You will be a perpetual student under the ongoing tutelage of Almighty God.

Your time on earth is limited, as was Jesus', and there is so much at stake. The lives of millions rest on the obedient few – the faithful remnant who will carry forth God's message and stand firm in His Truth. Prayer will be your tool to receive and understand the Lord's direction, and to discern His voice. Prayer will be your greatest secret weapon against the enemy.

Pray without ceasing (see 1 Thessalonians 5:17), and do not fall asleep while you're on your knees. Be alert. The enemy is waiting to catch you snoozing, and the Lord does not want to find you asleep when He returns. "Wake up!" He tells the church in Sardis (Revelation 3:2a). Review Luke 12:35-48, which is the record of Jesus' careful and explicit instruction to His disciples regarding the importance of watchfulness.

God is watching you, so be ever on the lookout for Him. How many wonderful ways has He shown Himself to you in the last few days of your fast? Praise Him that you forever remain in His all-seeing, unsleeping vision.

Dinner

"Come and have breakfast."
(John 21:12a)

⚜ **Daily Bread** – Read: John 21:1-19

So much of Christ's love and character is exhibited in these few verses of tonight's Daily Bread Scripture. They provide a perfect outline of God's revelations during these past 40 days.

Tomorrow, you will break your fast and dine with your family, but, tonight, one more time, let us join Jesus at the water's edge and return to the place where the disciples' journey began. Our Teacher awaits.

1. Jesus will take you back to the place He first met you (see Matthew 4:18 and John 21:1). In bringing you full circle, He gives you a clear picture of who you were and who He wants you to be. He does not want you to return to your old ways. You are a new person; He desires that you confront the old you and say "goodbye" once and for all.

2. God shows Himself to be the same yesterday, today, and forever. The same God who meets you on the stormy sea is the One who also meets you at the water's edge. While He finds great pleasure in your joy of reuniting with Him, He calls you to remember that He has always been there, and you should never again take your eyes off of Him (see Matthew 14:29 and John 21:7).

3. He provides all of your needs – and exceeds them – if you believe Him for them. Remember that He once asked the disciples to feed the multitude, and, though the source of their provision was right in front of their eyes, they were too blind to see it (see Matthew 14:16-17). At this subsequent breakfast reunion with His disciples, the Lord again provided fish and bread (see John 21:13), and the disciples' fishing nets were full with the bounty of their catch. God wants you to know that wherever He calls you to go, whatever He calls you to do, He will provide the necessary resources; just remember and acknowledge that He is the source of all your needs. As the disciples learned, when God asks you to feed the multitudes who are starving to know the risen Lord, you will be feeding them from an amply supply of God's grace.

4. Regardless of the depths of your sin, Christ will always restore you. No sin is too great for His forgiveness. The Lord's love is too great; He will never abandon nor forsake you (see Deuteronomy 31:6, Joshua 1:5, and Hebrews 13:5). Peter thought he had so greatly disappointed the Lord through his three denials of Christ (see Matthew 26:69-75) that he would be of no further use to Him, and he returned to his old lifestyle. But, Jesus met Peter exactly where he was, in the pit of his despair, and lifted his downcast soul. Peter covered himself in his shame, but he still presented himself before the Lord. Jesus gently removed Peter's disgrace as He restored him, forgave him, and cleansed him from every one of his denials. Jesus also confirmed His great love for Peter by telling him that he was still useful and that there remained a very specific plan and purpose for his life. Peter's Divine mission entrusted him with the care and feeding of all sheep belonging to the King of Kings (John 21:15-19).

In these four lessons, God illustrates His plan for all of His believers. First, He tells us to follow Him. Then, He cautions us to be watchful. Last, and certainly not least, He commissions us to go!

You've just met the Lord for breakfast tonight as you prepare to break your fast tomorrow morning. He has given you the necessary nourishment to begin your journey, and He will continue to sustain you along the way. You've spent so much time learning from Him, and you've developed the important habit of spending time alone with Him. You were a diligent student (weren't you?!) and recorded incredible and personal insights from His daily lessons.

Now that He has prepared and equipped you, He is sending you out as His representative. The Lord Jesus Christ commands you to embrace the Great Commission and to spread His renown to a hungering and thirsting world. You are to teach others about His great love; they are literally dying to meet Him. Go forth and show others how to know Him as intimately as you have been privileged to know Him. Take courage and do not be afraid. You know that He is leading you; He is your guiding Light.

Beloved, reflect on all that you have learned. Remember all the places the Lord has taken you. Record all the things that He has shown you. Recognize the very special and personal mission He has given you. Each of His children has a noble calling; if we're willing to fulfill it, He will gladly to show us the way.

If He has made His calling clear in your life, write it down, and rejoice! If He has just revealed the first step you are to take, or if you are still unsure about God's plan for your life, take time to journal right now, while your experience is still fresh. Later, when His plan is clear, you will have a reference point upon which to reflect. Your God is awesome and faithful, and a new chapter in your adventurous walk with Christ is just beginning.

Now, go in peace and serve the Lord. Thanks be to God!

Conclusion

"Every day they continued to meet together in the temple courts. They broke bread in their homes and ate together with glad and sincere hearts, praising God and enjoying the favor of all the people. And the Lord added to their number daily those who were being saved."
(Acts 2:46-47)

It is difficult to call this a conclusion; that word seems so final. What you've just experienced is not the end but the beginning of something much more. The Lord led you through some joyous times as well as a few difficult moments. You've been challenged and encouraged, confused and inspired, broken and healed, but, throughout it all, you've never been without the loving arms of Your Heavenly Father wrapped securely around you.

Whatever you have gleaned from this pilgrimage, it is very important to write it down because God plans to use it. Whatever He does in you and through you is for His glory. Before the beginning of the world, He planned for you to be at this exact place with Him at this precise time.

God specifically purposed and planned what you've learned during these 40 days in order to prepare you for the coming months and years ahead. He does not waste a single moment, and this precious time you shared with Him was provided by His gracious design. Since the fall of man in the Garden of Eden, God has focused on bringing His children back into a right and holy relationship with Him. And, here you are, at what has probably been one of the most intimate experiences in your Christian journey so far. Hopefully, you are now more profoundly in love with your Savior than you ever dreamed possible and are experiencing a depth of love you never before fathomed.

While you may have learned much, God's greatest hope is that you discovered the importance of abiding in Him. He is your first and foremost priority, forever, with no exception. Your Father has longed for a deep, abiding relationship with you. He wants to kindle your passion until you are burning to do His will. Great adventures await.

It is, as it always has been, for the good of His great Kingdom plan that you join Him at His table. As you rise from your place of safety and comfort to go out into the world and do the work that He has prepared for you, do not forget that you have a permanent reservation at His Divine table, and He longs to meet again. He extended you an open invitation, and He would love for you to bring a friend. He will be waiting when you return.

What you've learned should be shared, and, just as the first church was built by eating together in one another's homes, God intends for you to continue the same tradition. The Dutch have a word that describes a family living in harmony; it is "gezellig"; I believe that is how the Lord would like to see His church defined. His desire is that we are unified (Romans 15:5-6); we were never meant to compete or undermine each other. We were designed to uphold and encourage one another. He intended for us to work together to spread the good news of His coming. His desire is that we first love Him and then love another (Mark 12:29-31). Now that you've experienced deep, abiding love with your Father, you can better understand and appreciate what loving one another really requires.

The Lord has called you to cry out on behalf of your country and your world. He now asks you to serve as His ambassador, spreading His love throughout your sphere of influence. For the past 40 days, you depended on Him for every morsel; He will continue to nourish and sustain you, as long as you show up at His table. Now, return His favor, and invite Him to join you for each breakfast that you quietly eat in your car on the way to work, for each lunch that you share with your co-workers and friends, and for each dinner that you enjoy with your family. In every opportunity and every encounter, you represent Christ. Stand with assurance that He is right beside you, and living inside you, as you obediently share His amazing grace in your life.

The Lord has shown you great love in ways you never thought possible, and it should be your deepest desire to share that love with everyone He brings across your path. Jesus said, *"My command is this: Love each other as I have loved you. Greater love has no one than this, that he lay down his life for his friends. You are my friends if you do what I command."* (John 15:12-14).

You fully surrendered your life at the feet of Jesus. Now, you must go in His name to stake His claim for a lost and dying world. It's easy to fall right back into your old habits. As God takes you out of your comfort zone and into some unknown territory, your former life may seem comfortable and familiar in comparison, but do not make the mistake of regressing. Do not end where you began.

If you've learned anything these past few weeks, it is this: when God calls you, trust Him. When He asks *"Whom shall I send?"*, obediently and confidently say, *"Here am I. Send me."* (See Isaiah 6:8).

You have been the honored guest at the table of the King of Kings. You have tasted and seen just how good the Lord is. You have learned what it means to feast, rather than fast, and you have been satisfied, sustained, refreshed and filled with the richest of fare from the Lord's banqueting table. Now, Go! Share what you have learned with another hungry, starving soul and always remember that your place is reserved at the table of the King. May you never forget the intimacy you have found with the Lord as you have soaked in His Presence and in the power of His Word these past 40 days, and may an insatiable hunger to know the Lord more deeply and intimately draw you back to His table each and every day from this moment forward.

"The LORD bless you and keep you; the LORD make His face shine upon you and be gracious to you; the LORD turn His face toward you and give you peace."
(Numbers 6:24-26).

"So do not fear, for I am with you; do not be dismayed for I am your God. I will strengthen you and help you; I will uphold you with my righteous right hand."
(Isaiah 41:10).

My Fasting Resolution
The End of My Fast

Heavenly Father, 40 days have passed. My original commitment at the beginning of this journey was based solely on faith for where You would take me, Lord, and, now, here I am, completely amazed at Your faithfulness. The contrast of where I started and where I ended is living proof evidencing what You can do with a believer who is willing to take You at Your word.

Testimony of my 40 days with the Lord:

_____
_____
_____
_____
_____
_____
_____
_____
_____
_____
_____
_____
_____
_____
_____
_____
_____
_____
_____
_____
_____
_____

Heavenly Father, what You have begun in me, I pray to continue. I know I have a place to go and a purpose to fulfill. I realize that this journey was not intended to be an accomplishment but, rather, an establishment of the work You've prepared for me. Sharpen my mind, Lord, soften my heart, and open my eyes to all that you have planned for me. As You enabled me to trust You to fill my plate for every spiritual meal, help me continue to walk in faith, one step at a time.

I am full, Lord, and I do not ever want to be empty again.

Signature: _____

Date: _____

- APPENDIX B -

Fasting 101
A Brief Overview of Biblical Fasting

*"**When you fast**, do not look somber as the hypocrites do,*
For they disfigure their faces to show men they are fasting…
*But **when you fast**, put oil on your head and wash your face…"*
(Matthew 6:16-18)

The purpose of fasting is to lead us into deeper intimacy with, and dependence upon, the Lord as we seek His will for our life. Notice in Matthew that the Lord did not say "*if* you fast", He purposefully said, "*when you fast*" because He expects His followers to fast. In His Word, Jesus not only declared *that we would* fast, but, He also expressed *when we should* fast: **"The time will come when the bridegroom will be taken from them; then they will fast"** (Matthew 9:15b). Fasting involves surrendering the flesh to be renewed in the Spirit. When our Lord Jesus Christ ascended to the Father He sent His Holy Spirit to dwell within us to comfort us, guide us, and help us to experience the fullness of the abundant new life that our Savior laid down His life on the cross to give us. Fasting provides believers the opportunity to open the door and allow the Lord to come in and *eat* with us (reference Revelation 3:20) and experience the extraordinary privilege of soaking in God's Presence as we feast on the richest of fare, His Holy Word (reference Isaiah 55:1-2). Fasting allows the believer to be filled with God's holy and sustaining Word so they can be fueled to do the will of God.

When we fast unto the Lord, we can easily become distracted and consumed with the legalism of sacrificing our physical food. Our goal, however, when we come to the Lord in the spirit of fasting, is to separate ourselves from the distractions of this temporal world to allow God the opportunity to speak to us. Through the discipline of fasting we learn to redirect our focus off of the physical and onto the spiritual. When we fast we become completely dependent upon the Lord for all our needs, even our most basic necessity, food, so that He can teach us to depend on Him and in turn receive the direction, strength, and guidance we need to accomplish the work He is calling us to do in this world. If we are willing, the Lord will teach us, as He did the Israelites during their forty year wandering in the desert, **"that man does not live on bread alone but on every word that comes from the mouth of the LORD"** (Deuteronomy 8:3b).

Fasting is an act of consecration to God. It is a step of obedience and an act of worship. Through the discipline of fasting we are preparing and purifying our hearts to be more fully consecrated to the Lord. Repentance plays a primary role in the purification process as the Lord washes us with His life-giving water through the Word (reference Ephesians 5:26); cleansing us from areas of un-confessed sin and un-forgiveness that have been hindering our prayer life. Fasting removes those obstacles that have hindered us from being wholeheartedly surrendered to God and clears the channels so that His best blessings can more freely flow into our lives. Each time we submit to the Lord with prayer and fasting we grow, not only, in our knowledge of Him, but, we also experience a deeper passion for Him as our heart becomes more in tune with His. Our spiritual hearing also becomes more fine-tuned as we learn to discern His voice more clearly; and our desire to please Him takes priority as, we are no longer encumbered with the distractions of this world and our own fleshly impulses, instead, we are set free to respond more readily to His will. **"…and His sheep follow Him because they know His voice"** (John 10:4b).

Biblical Examples of Fasting:

When the men and women of the Bible sought the Lord with fasting and prayer they did so knowing they were powerless apart from God's Word being activated in their lives. When confronted with impossible and overwhelming circumstances fasting provided them the opportunity to shut out the opposing voices and become still before the Lord so they could discern His voice (reference 2 Chronicles 20:3-22). Fasting opens up the doorway to receive the necessary confirmation, encouragement, and confidence they needed to be the vessel God would use to accomplish His will.

⚜ **MOSES** – He fasted 40 days with no food or water, and returned to the mountain for another 40 days after the disobedience of the Israelites (Exodus 34:28) – His obedience led to the giving of the Law.

⚜ **ELIJAH** – He fasted for 40 days (1 Kings 19:8) – He was called to anoint a new generation of leaders after confronting the idolatry of the nation and calling the people to chose whom they would serve.

⚜ **NEHEMIAH** – He was so overcome by the destruction of his homeland that he could only respond with fasting and mourning (Nehemiah 1:3-4) – the Lord prepared him to make his request of the king to go and rebuild the walls of Jerusalem.

⚜ **ESTHER** – She, her maids, and the nation of Israel fasted 3 days with no food or water (Esther 4:16). She was given boldness and courage to go before the king and save her people from annihilation and her people were prepared to defend themselves.

⚜ **DANIEL** – He and his 3 friends fasted for 10 days on vegetables and water (Daniel 1:12) and were found to be ten times better in every matter of wisdom and understanding. Later, he fasted for 21 days with no choice food, meat, wine or lotions (Daniel 10:2-3) and his prayers helped overcome resistance of spiritual forces and he was given a prophetic vision.

⚜ **JESUS** – He fasted 40 days without food before beginning His earthly ministry (Matthew 4:2; Luke 4:2) and rebuked the devil with the Word of God and ultimately overcame the power of sin and death by accomplishing the greatest work in all human history by laying down His life and shedding His blood for the salvation of mankind! He set for us the ultimate example of the necessity of complete dependence upon the Father.

TYPES OF FASTS:

⚜ **THE NORMAL FAST** – No solid food is consumed; you may partake of liquids such as water, clear broths and juices. Jesus fasting for 40 days on water only is an example of a normal fast (Matthew 4:2).

Note: For the first few days of your fast you will have normal hunger pains and food cravings, but after about 3 days your body will begin to adjust to this new routine. Do not give into temptation, but feast more fully on the Word as your spiritual nourishment to sustain you where your physical food cannot. As you continue your fast for an extended period your body will become weak as it begins to eliminate toxins and wastes. This happens around week 1 and 2. It is important to adjust your schedule and get the rest your body needs as it is processing wastes and beginning to shut down certain functions in your body. This is a good time to press in to the Lord and rest in Him and begin to focus more fully on your new routine of spending time with the Lord during those normal meal times. As you continue into weeks 4 through 6 you will begin to experience a new found strength as your body has adjusted, eliminated wastes, and your mind becomes more clear and your hearing more in tune to the voice of God. It is a supernatural process that the Lord takes us through if we are willing to trust Him to lead us and sustain us in a way we have never experienced before. *"I can do everything through Him who gives me strength" (Philippians 4:13).*

⚜ **THE ABSOLUTE FAST** – (also called the Complete Fast) – In this fast no food or water is taken for a specified period of time. This type of fast is rare or limited for 1 to 3 days because the body cannot go without water beyond 3 days. Examples of this type of fast are found in Elijah (1 Kings 19:8); Ezra (Ezra 10:6); Esther (Esther 4:16) and Saul of Tarsus (Acts 9:9). Moses completed two 40 day absolute fasts – this was a supernatural fast only accomplished through the power of God. Moses was called by God and equipped by God for such a holy task.

⚜ **THE PARTIAL FAST** – This fast emphasizes restricting one's diet by eliminating certain foods (such as no sweets, no fast foods, no meat, etc.), or restricting or eliminating certain meals for a part of a day or week on a rotational basis (i.e. only eating 1 meal a day). Examples of this type of fast are found in Elijah when fed by ravens and the widow of Zarephath (1 Kings 17:6; 15); and Daniel who ate only vegetables and drank water (Daniel 1:15: 10:3). This fast may seem the simplest at first, but it requires no less discipline than the others and can be a stepping stone to undertaking a Normal Fast.

Before you begin your fast it is important to pray and ask the Lord to reveal to you the type of fast and the duration of the fast He is calling you to do. It is recommended that you consult a medical professional if you have specific medical conditions or take prescribed medication before beginning a fast of any length. For people of normal health the partial or Daniel-type fast is recommended when using any of the prayer and fasting devotionals available through Trumpet and Torch Ministries. The Daniel Fast, as taken from the Scriptures in Daniel chapter one, describes a diet of vegetables and water, or whole grain and organic foods (the emphasis for the modern times we live in is on eliminating processed foods and caffeine to partake of a more wholesome organic diet that will lead to a healthy lifestyle change). It is a good idea to begin eliminating caffeine and processed sugars a few days before beginning your fast. When you are ready to end your fast it is important to let your body adjust slowly to returning to a normal eating schedule by taking in only broths to begin and adding one food at a time – you should return to a normal eating schedule within a week (hopefully by the end of your fast you've successfully eliminated those unhealthy choices you've been making over the years and are committed to maintaining a more healthy lifestyle – both physically and spiritually!)

TRUE FASTING

The type of fast the Lord calls all believers to, as outlined in the Book of Isaiah, Chapter 58, is a call to obedience and action. Fasting is not about proving to yourself or to anyone else that you can accomplish such a spiritual feat. Fasting is about our worship and devotion to God. If done with the proper motivation fasting can be very beneficial to the body, mind and spirit. Most medical professionals would agree that fasting helps to restore the body to a more natural and healthy state.

This ministry encourages believers to focus more on "feasting" on the Word of God as you begin to surrender your busy schedule to spending more time with the Lord. While you may be adjusting your physical meals during your fast it is vital that you don't miss any spiritual meals as you learn to dine with the Lord in prayer and feast upon His Word three times a day. Your physical and fleshly appetite for the artificial and unhealthy substitutes of the world will begin to be replaced with a growing hunger for the more satisfying and fulfilling things of God.

All believers can answer the call to fast and everyone can eliminate unnecessary foods and pleasures that are keeping them from spending more intimate time with the Lord in His Word and prayer. If fear of not eating is preventing you from even taking this step of faith, this ministry recommends that you use the EAT at the Table of the King devotional and come to the Lord with an offering of your time and allow Him to do the necessary cutting and eliminating as you trust Him to fill you with His Word each day and each meal. You will find as you spend this time with Him each day that He will give you the strength and desire to sacrifice yourself more fully as time goes by. ***"To obey is better than sacrifice"*** (1 Samuel 15:22). He is looking for you to trust Him and His desire is not to harm you but to give you a future and a hope (reference Jeremiah

29:11-13). He wouldn't lead us where He hasn't been Himself and He knows the benefits far outweigh the painful process that it takes to get us to that finish line!

It is recommended that you keep a daily journal of your journey with the Lord. Begin by submitting your questions, concerns and requests to the Lord and wait upon Him to reveal His will and purpose for your life as you take this step of obedience. Be willing to address those areas of sin and unforgiveness that are hindering your prayers and preventing you from fully hearing the voice of God.

WHY FAST FOR 40 DAYS?

Throughout Scripture we find that forty days is God's divine period of time to accomplish His redemptive work in the world. We find examples of this with Noah and the flood (Genesis 7:4), Moses and the Law (Deuteronomy 9:11), Elijah and the restoration (1 Kings 19:8; Malachi 4:4-6; Mark 9:2); Jonah and the revival of Nineveh (Jonah 3:1-10), and Jesus and salvation (Matthew 4:2). The Lord can accomplish in 40 days what can often take a lifetime by human standards. If He can transform nations in this time frame consider what He can do with your heart. He desires whole-hearted devotion from His followers. When we answer His call to fast He is giving each of us an opportunity to be proactive in this spiritual war that we are all participants in, whether we like it or not. We have a divine responsibility to respond to His call and allow Him to do the necessary work to cut out of our lives those fleshly and unhealthy things that are keeping us from being fully His. When we submit to a period of 40 days of fasting and prayer we allow Him the necessary time and attention to do an extraordinary work *in* our lives to prepare us for what He purposes to do *through* our lives to reach and bless the world with His forgiveness and salvation. Fasting puts us in a position to receive His power, presence, and provision to become the vessel He will use to accomplish His kingdom's work. May we not let our fears of the unknown be the thing that stops us from experiencing the wonders He has in store for us (Jeremiah 33:3). He is standing at the door and knocking waiting for us to come in and eat with Him (Revelation 3:20). Submit your fears, your questions, and your concerns to the One Who holds your life and future in His all-sufficient, all-powerful, and capable hands – He won't let you down; on the contrary, He wants to bless you in ways you have never known!

"My grace is sufficient for you,
For My power is made perfect in weakness."
(2 Corinthians 12:8)

HOW TO GET STARTED:

1. PRAY. Each journey will be unique to each individual – don't measure any part of your journey with another – God has something special just for you that He wants to do in and through your life. Submit your fears to the Lord and pray for direction before beginning your journey. **Ask Him to show you specifically the time frame and the type of fast He is calling you to do.** Throughout Scripture the duration of a fast aligned with the time frame necessary for the servant to be used of God (consider Esther fasting for 3 days and the three days of banquets before the request was granted (Esther 4:16; 5:4; 5:8; 7:1-4) or Daniel and his 3 friends who fasted for 10 days and were found to be 10 times better in knowledge and understanding in the whole kingdom (Daniel 1:12, 15, 20), and who later fasted for 21 days and was told that the archangel Michael was able to overcome the demonic force in the Persian realm after 21 days (Daniel 10:2-3; 13)). The Lord has a specific purpose for the fast He is calling you to – recording the specifics and then being obedient to His call is vital for what He desires to accomplish in and through your life.

2. EAT. Set aside worldly distractions to sit at the table of the King of the universe and spend intimate time with the Lord in prayer as He fills you and washes you and with water through His life-giving Word (Ephesians 5:26-27). The Word of God and Prayer are the two most important elements to a successful fasting journey. Without a daily diet of His Word you are simply dieting! A believer who is too busy to spend time in the Word or prayer is of no threat to Satan and of no use to the Kingdom of God. The Lord is looking for men and women who are willing to set aside temporal worldly pursuits and give themselves fully to the work of prayer so His power can be unleashed in the world reference Ezekiel 22:30). *"I tell you the truth, anyone who has faith in Me will do what I have been doing. He will do even greater things than these, because I am going to the Father. And I will do whatever you ask in My name, so that the Son may bring glory to the Father. You may ask Me for anything in My name, and I will do it"* (John 14:12-14). A daily diet of the Word of God will provide the nourishment and insight necessary to add fuel to our prayers!

3. BELIEVE God for one meal at a time and one day at a time. When your stomach begins to growl, consider it a signal from God to press in more fully and dine more heartily on His filling and sustaining Word. Allow the Lord to do the necessary stripping and cleansing as His "living and active" Word begins to take root in your life (Hebrews 4:12). Repentance is an important part of this journey – the Lord is jealous for you to be fully devoted and dependent upon Him and no other – we have forsaken our first Love and must return to Him with wholehearted devotion – He is jealous for us! (Exodus 34:14; 2 Chronicles 7:14; Revelation 2:4-5;).

4. REJOICE AND GIVE THANKS to the Lord for the work He is doing in and through your life and that He has personally called you to such an intimate place for such a time as this. He delights in your willingness and responsiveness to desire to spend time with Him as much as He longs to spend time with you! (Psalm 100; Luke 10:39-42).

Please visit www.trumpetandtorch.org for further resources and information on fasting and prayer and to participate in any one of our 3, 5, 7, 10, 12, and 40 day journeys. May your time of "feasting" open the door to experience the presence and power of God as you may have never known before, and may your relationship with the Lord be deeply enriched and your spiritual appetite be deeply satisfied as you seek Him in this way! *"Blessed are you who hunger now, for you will be satisfied"* (Luke 6:21a).

"My food," said Jesus, 'Is to do the will of Him Who sent Me and to finish His work."
(John 4:34)

- Appendix C -

♣ SOURCES

Unless otherwise indicated, all Scripture quotations are from the *Holy Bible, New International Version*, NIV, © 1973, 1978, 1984 International Bible Society. Scripture quotations identified KJV are from the *Holy Bible, King James Version*.

Additional Source Quotations from:

Famous Quotations Network (famous-quotations.com)
"Quotable Quotes" (Pleasantville, NY: The Reader's Digest Association, 1997).
Ten Boom, Corrie. *Each New Day.* (Grand Rapids, MI: Fleming H. Dewell, a division of Baker Book House Company, © 1977, 2003).
Ten Boom, Corrie. *Father Ten Boom: God's Man* (Old Tappan, NJ: Revell, 1978).
Ten Boom, Corrie. *Tramp for the Lord* (Fort Washington, PA: Christian Literature Crusade, 1974).
Ten Boom, Corrie. *In My Father's House* (Boston, MA: G.K. Hall, 1976).
Ten Boom, Corrie. *Not I, But Christ* (Nashville, TN: T. Nelson, 1984).
Carlson, Carole C. *Corrie ten Boom: Her Life Her Faith* (Old Tappan, N.J.: F.H. Revell Co., 1983).
Ten Boom, Corrie. *The Hiding Place* (New York, NY: Bantam, 1996).

- Appendix D -

RECOMMENDED BOOKS ON FASTING AND REVIVAL

Bragg, Paul C. and Patricia. *The Miracle of Fasting.* (Santa Barbara, CA: Health Science, n.d.).
Bright, Bill. *The Coming Revival.* (Orlando, FL: New Life Publications, 1995). See pages 131-135 for prayers of repentance).
Bright, Bill. *First Love.* (Orlando, FL: New Life Publications, 2002).
Bright, Bill. *The Transforming Power of Fasting and Prayer.* (Orlando, FL: New Life Publications, 1997).
Bright, Bill and Jenson, Ron. *Glow in the Dark.* (Sisters, OR: Multnomah Publishers, Inc., 2005).
Jonathan Edwards on Revival. (Carlisle, PA: The Banner of Truth Trust, 1987).
Towns, Elmer L. *Fasting for Spiritual Breakthrough.* (Ventura, CA: Regal Books, 1996).
Towns, Elmer L. *Knowing God Through Fasting.* (Shippensburg, PA: Destiny Image Publishers, Inc., 2002).
Wallis, Arthur. *God's Chosen Fast.* (Fort Washington, PA: Christian Literature Crusade, 1993).

- Appendix E -

NOTES

1 Ten Boom, Corrie, *Each New Day: 365 Simple Reflections*. (Grand Rapids, MI: Fleming H. Revell, a division of Baker Book House Company, 2003), p. 52.
2 Lewis, C.S. *Mere Christianity*. (New York, NY: Harper Collins, 1980), p.46.
3 Lewis, C.S. *The Chronicles of Narnia: The Lion, The Witch, and The Wardrobe*. (New York, NY: Harper Collins, 1954).
4 *2002 Personal Prayer Journal*, (Minneapolis, MN: World Wide Publications, 2001), p.31.
5 Ibid., p.9.
6 Brown, Catherine. *Confessions of a Fasting Housewife*. (Pescara, Italy: Destiny Image Europe, 2005), p. 89.
7 Carlson, Carole C. *Corrie ten Boom: Her Life, Her Faith*. (Fleming H. Revell Co., 1982), p.117.
8 Lucado, Max. *Experiencing the Heart of Jesus*. (Nashville, TN: Thomas Nelson, Inc., 2004), p. 197.
9 Moore, Beth. *The Patriarchs*. (Nashville, TN: LifeWay Press, 2005).
10 Gothard, Bill. *The Power of Spoken Blessings*. (Sisters, OR: Multnomah Publishers, 2004).
11 Grant, Natalie. *Awaken* Audio CD, "The Real Me" Track. (Curb Records, 2005).
12 Towns Elmer. Knowing God Through Fasting. (Shippensburg, PA: Destiny Image Publishers, Inc., 2002), p.89.
13 Stanley, Charles F. *When The Enemy Strikes*. (Nashville, TN: Thomas Nelson, Inc., 2004).
14 Carlson, Carole C. *Corrie ten Boom: Her Life, Her Faith*. (Fleming H. Revell Co., 1982), p.7.
15 Hall, Charlie. *Flying Into Daybreak* Audio CD, "Center" Track. (Six Step Records, 2006).
16 Gothard, Bill. *Institute in Basic Youth Conflicts Seminars*. (Eugene, OR: Institute in Basic Life Principles, 1982).
17 Graham, Billy. *Storm Warning*. (Word Publishing, 1992), p. 67.
18 Carlson, Carole C. *Corrie ten Boom: Her Life, Her Faith*. (Fleming H. Revell Co.,1982), p. 191.
19 Ibid., p. 30.

Additional Blank Journal Pages

Continue Your Journey

WITH THESE ADDITIONAL PRAYER AND FASTING DEVOTIONALS
BY TRACI A. ALEXANDER

WELLSPRING

⚜ Unleash Your Passion For God

The second in a series of 40-day fasting journeys, this is a vital and necessary next step to experience a life of full devotion with the Lord. Having our hearts opened and laid bare during our first 40 days we must be careful to learn to guard our heart and allow God to continue His refining process as He tranforms us into a useful vessel to be poured out as a drink offering on a dry and weary land.

HARVEST

The Kingdom of God ⚜

The third in a series of 40-day fasting journeys, this journey invites us to jouney with Jesus as He walks with His disciples during those important 40 days between His resurrection and ascension. This is a journey for all true followers of Jesus Christ as He prepares us to trust, wait and believe in His promised coming and our present calling as commisioned ministers of the gospel of grace to a lost and dying world.

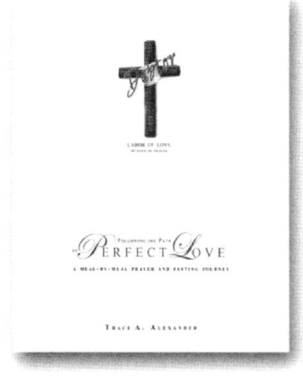

DEBTOR

⚜ Labor of Love

The fourth in a series of 40-day prayer and fasting journeys, this journey focuses on the high and holy calling of prayer in the life of the believer. There is no greater expression of love than the willingness to lay down one's life in prayer for another as Jesus so eloquently illustrated for us in His life on this earth. There is no greater work, and no greater deficit in the church, nor more difficult position to fill in all of God's kingdom, than to find faithful followers who are willing to stand in the gap and answer the call to pray.

VISIT WWW.TRUMPETANDTORCH.ORG TO ACCESS AND ORDER THESE AND OTHER DEVOTIONALS

THE FEAST OF TABERNACLES

✣ *An 8-day ordination ceremony*

The Lord calls us to be holy because He is holy. In this 8-day prayer and fasting devotional journey we will enter the Most Holy Place and experience what it means to be set apart and "Holy Unto the Lord." We have been called to be a kingdom of priests, for we are the temple of the Lord in which His presence dwells and through which He reveals Himself to the world. It is time we recognize the privileged position we have been granted and live the life of holiness He demands of His chosen saints.

THE FESTIVAL OF LIGHTS

✣ *An 8-day devotional email journey - Put on the Armor of Light*

An 8-day re-dedication ceremony commemorating the Jewish celebration of Hanukkah or "dedication" originally taken December 12-19, 2009. Join in the journey as we light the 9- branch Menorah utilizing the Fruit of the Spirit to guide us as we rededicate our lives as the temple of God and consecrate our hearts to our holy call to reveal the light of Christ to the lost and fallen world.

EPHIPHANY

✣ *Our Coming King!*

A 12-day devotional email journey following the birth of our Savior as we prepare for the year ahead with our eyes fixed and hearts prepared to worship and receive our reigning and coming King! Join us as we unveil and reveal the wisdom, work, worship, witness, wealth, will, wrath, way, wait, word, watch, and wonder of God. This journey was originally taken at Christmas 2008 through the Epiphany in January 2009.

VISIT WWW.TRUMPETANDTORCH.ORG TO ACCESS AND ORDER THESE AND OTHER DEVOTIONALS

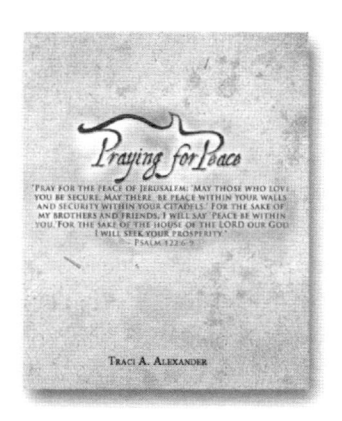

Praying for Peace
✣ *10-days of Prayer for the Peace of Israel*

10-day prayer journey to pray for the peace of Israel as we walk through God's covenant commands for His holy people and recommit ourselves to a life of obedience and faithfulness to remain committed to His Word and devoted in prayer for His kingdom to come and His will to be done on this earth as it is in heaven. This journey was originally taken following our Journey to the Holy Land - June 1-10, 2009.

Journey to the Holy Land
✣ *A 10-day devotional Pilgrimage to the Holy Land*

Traveling to the Holy Land was the trip of a lifetime - I invite you to join me on my own personal pilgrimage to the land of the Bible and walk the path that Jesus walked during His own earthly pilgrimage as He fulfilled the will of the Father. The Bible comes to life after you have walked this amazing journey. May your heart be set on fire for Israel and may you join us in prayer as we pray for the peace of Israel.

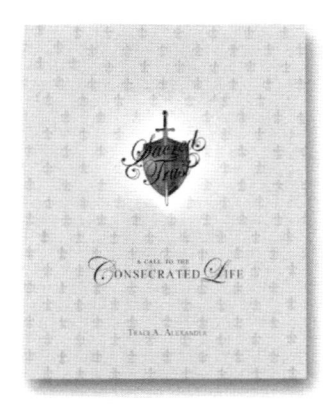

Sacred Trust
✣ *A Call to the Consecrated Life*

We have been given a Sacred Trust as the children of God to "Consecrate [our]selves and be holy, because [He] is holy" (Leviticus 11:44).
This 10-day (Daniel-fast) journey issues a trumpet wake-up call and warning to the Church and challenges believers, through a time of testing and recommittment, to address the sin that has paralyzed the Church, poisoned our prayer life, and rendered us ineffective in impacting the world for the glory of God.

VISIT WWW.TRUMPETANDTORCH.ORG TO ACCESS AND ORDER THESE AND OTHER DEVOTIONALS

CRUCIFIED
♣ A 40 day prayer and fasting journey - Revealing the Wisdom and Power of God.

The fifth in a series of meal-by-meal prayer and fasting journeys, CRUCIFIED, reveals the person and work of Jesus Christ and His utmost desire for our lives - to know Him. We have been called, not to a cause, but to a person - Jesus Christ, and like the apostle Paul our highest pursuit should be to proclaim nothing else but Christ and Him Crucified. Journey back to the place it all began and experience the power and wisdom of God in the message of the cross.

VISIT WWW.TRUMPETANDTORCH.ORG TO ACCESS AND ORDER THESE AND OTHER DEVOTIONALS